TB MINAR QUTB

B HUMAYUN'S TOM

RT AGRA FO RA F

TAJ MA AJ M

IKRI UR SI

I SANCH SANCHI

HAJURAHO KHA

TA ELEPHANTA

TA CAVES AJANTA CAV

LLORA CAVES ELL

OLD GOA OLD

DAKAL PATTADAKAL

AMPI HAMPI HA

BRIHADISVARA

AMALLAPURAM MAM

RAK KONARAK

ALAYAN RAILWAY

ƒ 1,50

TRAVEL GUIDE
A Good Earth Publication

Speaking Stones

World Cultural Heritage Sites in India

EICHER GOODEARTH LIMITED, New Delhi

Supported by

Department of Tourism, Government of India

A GOOD EARTH PUBLICATION

ISBN 81-87780-00-2

Editor and Publisher: Swati Mitra

Designer: Sagarmoy Paul
Senior Editor: Sona Thakur

Photographs:
Benoy K Behl (pp. 12Middle, 154-59, 163-66, 167Above, 168-69, 170-77, 178A, 179, 182, 183Below)
Ranjan De (pp.12A, 199, 201B, 205B)
Shilbhadra Dutta (pp. 11, 17, 212A, 218A, 219M, 221, 224, 229, 231)
Shalinee Ghosh (pp. 26)
Swati Mitra (pp. 9B, 10, 15B, 92, 94, 98 A&B, 99, 100-4, 106-9, 112B, 113, 122-31, 132-41, 142-46, 151, 152A, 153, 160, 162, 167B, 178B, 180A, 183A, 184-95, 204A, 206 A&B)
Salim Paul (pp. 196-98, 201A, 202-203, 204B, 205A&M, 207)
Varsha Rani (pp. 60-61, 90-91, 95-97, 98M, 105, 110, 112A, 147-148)
Surendra Sahai (pp. 6, 13, 16, 18-25, 28-33, 34-45, 56, 58, 62, 64, 66, 109B, 208-209, 210A, 211, 212B, 215, 218B)
Mohit Saxena (pp. 46-55, 65, 68-89)
Harsh Vardhan (pp. 222, 226, 228, 230)

Text:
Bill Aitken, Annabel Lopez,
M N Rajesh, Subhadra Sengupta, Sona Thakur, Varsha Rani
Maps & Drawings: V Murali
Secretarial Assistance: Leela Sarna
Architectural Illustrations: Himanish Das (pp. 20 & 36)

The Publishers would be happy to receive suggestions and corrections for inclusion in the next edition. Please write to
Head of Publishing, Eicher Goodearth Ltd, Eicher House,
12 Commercial Complex, Greater Kailash II (Masjid Moth), New Delhi 110 048.
PIC No 01111

This publication has been supported by
Department of Tourism, Government of India

Printed by Ajanta Offset & Packaging Ltd, New Delhi
on behalf of Eicher Goodearth Ltd

Price: Rs 270

Contents

World Heritage Cultural Sites

In 1972, the United Nations Educational, Scientific and Cultural Organisation (UNESCO) launched a programme for the identification, protection and preservation of cultural and natural Heritage Sites across the world.

The cultural sites include monuments with historical, aesthetic, archaeological, scientific, ethnological or anthropological value.
A site was deemed of national heritage by virtue of its 'outstanding universal value'.

To qualify for the World Heritage List, a site should:

- represent a masterpiece of human creative genius
- exhibit an important interchange of human values over a span of time or within a cultural area, or developments in architecture or technology
- bear a unique or at least exceptional testimony to a cultural tradition or a civilisation
- be an outstanding example of a type of building or architectural or technological ensemble or landscape which illustrates a significant stage in history
- be an outstanding example of a traditional human settlement or land-use, especially when it has become vulnerable under the impact of irreversible change
- be directly or tangibly associated with events or living traditions, with ideas or beliefs, or with artistic and literary works of universal significance

WORLD HERITAGE CULTURAL SITES IN INDIA

1. Qutb Minar
2. Humayun's Tomb
3. Agra Fort
4. Taj Mahal
5. Fatehpur Sikri
6. Sanchi
7. Khajuraho
8. Elephanta Cave
9. Ajanta Caves
10. Ellora Caves
11. Old Goa
12. Pattadakal
13. Hampi
14. Brihadisvara
15. Mamallapuram
16. Konarak
17. Darjeeling Himalayan Railway

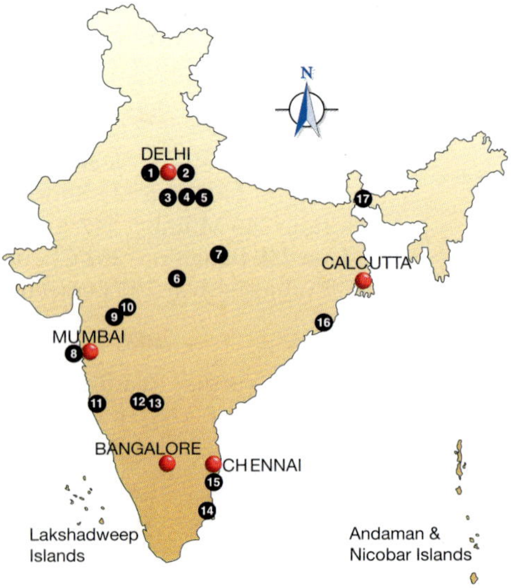

About the Guide

This book takes you on a tour of the World Heritage Cultural Sites in India. The itinerary that we have proposed does not follow the sites in a historical or chronological sequence. Instead, we have grouped the sites in a sequence that is the most practical from the traveller's point of view.

The four metropolitan cities of Delhi, Mumbai, Bangalore and Chennai have been identified as gateways for a group of sites closest to them. For instance, Delhi is the most convenient base not just for the two Heritage Sites in the city, Qutb Minar and Humayun's Tomb, but also for the sites in Agra, Fatehpur Sikri, Sanchi and Khajuraho.

The book brings to life the Heritage Sites with specially commissioned photographs and detailed site maps. The vivid narrative brings out the historical and architectural importance of these monuments.

The **Practical Information** section at the end of the book provides all the information a traveller may need from the time he decides to come to India. It includes comprehensive and up-to-date details of visas and permits, travel and banking.

The **Travellers' Needs** section has been arranged sequentially for the ease of the traveller. The sites have been divided into mini-circuits, each grouped around a metropolis as the most convenient base. Details of transportation, tourist offices and hotels at the sites, as well as the access cities, have been compiled after actually visiting each site.

A comprehensive **Phrase Book** from English to Hindi helps the foreign traveller cope with travels in an alien land. A detailed **Glossary** explains Indian words as well as unfamiliar architectural terms.

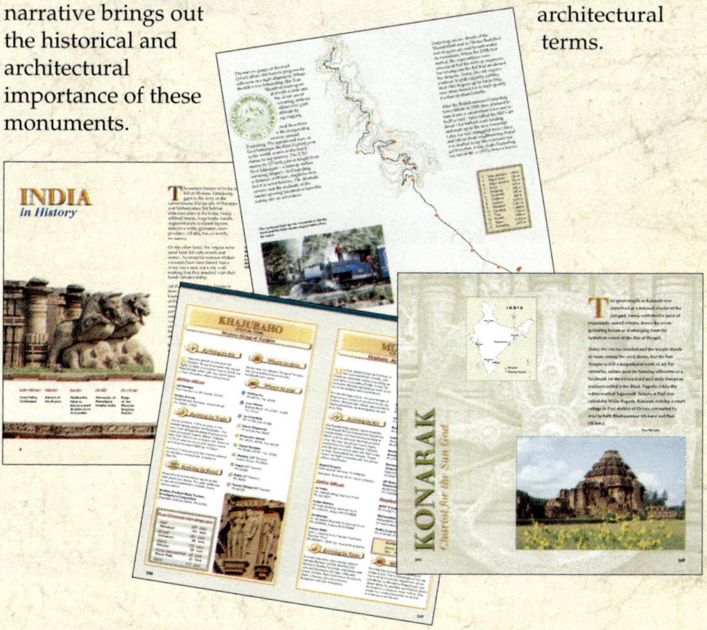

INDIA
in History

2500-1900 BC	1500 BC	566 BC	326 BC	273-236 BC
Indus Valley Civilisation	**Advent of the Aryans**	**Siddhartha, later to become Lord Buddha, born in Lumbini**	**Alexander of Macedonia invades India**	**Reign of the Mauryan Emperor Ashoka**

The earliest history of India is full of silences. Tantalising gaps in the story of the subcontinent. The people of Harappa and Mohenjodaro left behind elaborate cities in the Indus Valley – cobbled streets, huge baths, canals, engraved seals, sculpted figures, defensive walls, granaries, even jewellery. All this, but no words, no names.

On the other hand, the Aryans who came later, left only words and names. No material remains of their existence have been found. Not a stone, not a seal, not a city wall: nothing that they touched with their hands remains today.

All that we know of the Aryans is from the *Vedas*, their hymnal books of knowledge. Piecing together a picture of their world from their words, we come to know that they were a patriarchal people; their gods were anthropomorphic, and ritual sacrifice was the essence of their spiritual identity. They knew of gold and of bronze, they built with wood and measured wealth in cattle.

But the earliest archaeological evidence of the early Aryan migrants – some shards of painted grayware excavated from Hastinapura in North India – date only to 1000 BC.

Left:
Sun Temple at Konarak, 13th century

Below:
Bronze dancing girl from Mohenjodaro, 2500 BC

150 BC	**77 AD**	**335-455 AD**	**629-645 AD**	**640-690 AD**
***Stupas* at Sanchi**	**Kanishka the Kushan ascends throne**	**Golden age of the Guptas**	**Chinese traveller Hiuen Tsang in India**	**Pallavas build at Mamallapuram**

The half-millenium before that which the Aryans had already spent in the land-that-would-be-India, remains unchronicled. So, like the *Vedas* themselves, early Indian history too is essentially *shruti*, wisdom received by the ears.

It is only with the Buddhists that history becomes tangible and tactile. The *stupas* of Sanchi and Barhut are the first complete impressions of the land the Aryans colonised.

Gautama Buddha in Gandhara style, 2nd-3rd century BC

Newer waves of migration from the West pushed the early settlers eastwards. These were fertile lands and, slowly, the Aryans gave up their nomadic-pastoral way of life and settled down to farming. Soon, they had enough surplus produce to fuel urbanisation, structured administration, industry and trade. And gradually, as this process snowballed, there emerged organised states, both monarchical and republican.

The Aryans moved out of the *saptasindhu*, the basin of the Indus and its tributaries, along two routes: The *uttarapatha* that shadowed the Ganga eastward and the *dakshinapatha*, which swung southward in a great arc, before heading towards the western coast.

500-757 AD	8th century	1010 AD	1192 AD	1199 AD
Chalukyas of Badami	Kailasa Temple at Ellora	Rajaraja Chola builds Brihadisvara Temple	Mohammed Ghuri attacks Delhi	First storey of Qutb Minar built

These axes of migration, the *uttarapatha* and the *dakshinapatha*, also became the routes for trade and transit, and for Buddhist proselytism. They also became the axis for much of architecture and sculpture, the two signposts of Indian history.

Left:
Detail from the Great Stupa at Sanchi, c 150 BC

For five centuries after the collapse of the Mauryan empire in 184 BC, even as dynasties were spawning and disintegrating, the trading class grew from wealth to wealth, ferrying goods to and from the mighty empires of Rome, Greece and China. So it followed that Buddhism, primarily the religion of the merchant class, also flourished, for it denied taboos on food and travel which made trade so cumbersome for the Brahamanical orthodoxy.

The series of rock-cut caves found in central India, for instance, exist almost entirely due to the munificence of these merchants. Situated for the major part on the *dakshinapatha* as it veered to the ports of the western coast, the caves offered the traders sanctuaries and shrines to retreat into while they plied their wares.

Below:
Pillar from Indrasabha cave at Ellora, 800-1100 AD

1498 AD	1509-1529 AD	1510 AD	1526 AD	1556-1605 AD
Vasco da Gama lands at Calicut	**Krishna Deva Raya rules Hampi**	**Alphonso de Albuquerque captures Goa**	**Babur becomes the first Mughal emperor**	**Reign of Akbar**

The years between 300-500 AD, corresponding roughly to the unifying reign of the Gupta dynasty, are generally termed the classical age of North India. It was during this period of political stability that an ordered socio-cultural matrix – including art and music, literature and language – was forged. The cave paintings of Ajanta, the dramatic compositions of Kalidasa, all touched inspiring levels in this epoch.

Boddhisattava Vajrapani from Cave I at Ajanta, 5th century AD

Besides the arts, seminal works on astronomy, medicine and mathematics were produced. This period saw the length of the solar year calculated with a precision attained not even by the Greeks, the decimal system perfected and the value of pi calculated to the fourth decimal point. It saw the appearance of the zero, albeit as a dot or *bindu*.

However, little survives of the architecture of this period. This architectural silence has often been ascribed to the demolishing instincts of the Muslim invaders from the north-west who began straying into India from the eighth century onward. Perhaps more pertinent is the fact that the buildings of this period were non-durable structures and were quickly built over when they fell into disuse.

1612 AD	1648 AD	1650 AD	1699 AD	1853 AD
English establish first factory at Surat	Shah Jahan builds his new citadel, Lal Qila, in Delhi	Taj Mahal completed	Gobind Singh, 10th Sikh guru, forms the Khalsa	Railways come to India; Bombay to Thane line laid

In fact, anyone studying the architecture of North India is struck by the fact that most of the ancient monuments that excite wonder were built not by the major dynasties, but by the minor figures of history. Important and long-reigning dynasties including the Kushanas, the Mauryas, and the Guptas did not leave architectural monuments, while minor players are remembered for the magnificent temples they left behind.

Left:
From Kandariya Mahadev Temple at Khajuraho, 1025-50 AD

The emergence of the temple in its glory in North India was, in fact, impelled by the rise of regional feudatory states from AD 700 to 1200 and was confined to isolated pockets like Khajuraho and Konarak.

Meanwhile in the South, the first century after the birth of Christ saw the emergence of a series of small kingdoms.

Below:
Chariot wheel from Sun Temple at Konarak, 13th century AD

1857 AD	1858 AD	1912 AD	1920 AD	1947 AD
Indian sepoys' rise against British rule	**British India under direct rule of the Crown**	**Imperial capital shifted to Delhi from Calcutta**	**Mahatama Gandhi launches non-cooperation movement**	**India gains Independence**

Shore Temple, Mamallapuram, 674-690 AD

In a pattern that persisted for almost a millenium, there was a see-sawing of dynasties fairly balanced in political and military strength. The Pallavas of Kanchipuram, the Cholas of Thanjavur, the Cheras, the Chalukyas, the Rashtrakutas, all lorded over the South at some point.

But even though there was little by way of political continuance, the South during these centuries seized the initiative of progress. Be it in local self-governance, or the evolution of devotional *bhakti* cults, or even the cementing of trade ties with Arab or Chinese merchants, it was southern India that surged ahead.

Right:
Dancing Shiva from Virupaksha Temple at Pattadakal, 745 AD

Below:
Bronze Nataraja of the late Chola period, 12th century

Along with the surplus wealth generated by a favourable balance of overseas trade, there was a resurgence of religiosity between the 5th and the 7th centuries as Brahmanism percolated southward. The worship of Shiva and Vishnu that had swamped the North for the past few centuries began to catch the imagination of the people, and more importantly, that of the kings of the South.

Royal devotion to the two Brahmanical gods led to huge temples being commissioned by several southern kings, including the Pallavas, the Chalukyas and the Cholas. In most cases the temples that were consecrated between the 8th and the 12th centuries are still flourishing today. This, perhaps, is the reason southern temples are better preserved than the temples of the North.

Back in the North, chronic fragmentation had made the subcontinent vulnerable to repeated incursions whenever the soldiers of Islam raised their swords in the service of Allah. After several rounds of hit-and-run raids on the subcontinent by assorted Turks and Afghans, Mohammed Ghuri in 1196 AD finally came to stay, ushering in six centuries of rule under various Turk, Afghan and, finally, Mongol dynasties.

Qutb Minar, 1199 AD

The architectural imprint of these regimes was a series of robust monuments done in a style that aimed for the classical Islamic, but achieved only a hybrid for it was executed by Hindu craftsmen unfamiliar with the model given to them.

At the turn of the 16th century, the entire subcontinent was divided and uncertain. The South was constantly warring, while the North was largely controlled by several dynasties of an alien religion.

The subcontinent had also turned into something of a lodestar for every enterprising or adventurous young man from the unsettled lands of Central Asia, Afghanistan and Iran. One such young prince rode into India from Samarkand and with a small force, ousted the Delhi Sultan after the Battle of Panipat in 1526. He established what came to be called the Mughal dynasty, which became a fact of India's political life and influenced its socio-cultural profile as it made the first attempt to integrate the subcontinent's disparate society.

Humayun's Tomb, c1560 AD

Akbar, the greatest of the great Mughals, rose from being just another Muslim king of Delhi to the Emperor of all Hindustan. He made the Mughals a part of the accepted order of things on the subcontinent.

Emperor Akbar supervising the building of Fatehpur Sikri

Shahjahan, 1628-1658 AD

Akbar's policies of martial and marital alliances with the Rajputs led to a greater interaction between the Hindus and the Muslims, making them far more willing to borrow from the other. Nowhere was this more evident than in the architecture of this period, a happy amalgam of the best of the Persian and classical Hindu styles.

Born out of Akbar's syncretic policies, this fusion style was perfected under Shahjahan, who inherited not only his grandfather's open-mindedness, but also his belief that building was an integral part of empire-building.

He marked up a tally of several elegant forts, palaces and mosques and even a whole new imperial city with processional thoroughfares, bazaars and cool waterways. Besides, of course, giving India the wondrous Taj Mahal.

St Francis Xavier, patron saint of Goa, 1506-1552 AD

Back in 1498, even before the Mughals appeared on the Indian landscape, Europe had forged its own passage to India, when the Portuguese Vasco da Gama landed at Calicut in search of spices and souls to save. Over the next century, the rest of western Europe followed, and the French, the Dutch and the British set up their respective trading posts on the subcontinent.

Mughal India traded with the Europeans, employed them and occasionally skirmished with them. In fact, the British East India Company spent its earliest years in India functioning much as a maritime auxiliary of the Mughal empire.

In fact, Sir Thomas Roe, the ambassador sent by the English king, James I, to Jahangir's court in 1618, actually extracted the *firman* (royal license) to trade from Jahangir in return for protecting Mughal commercial and Mecca-bound traffic from Portuguese raids. Gradually, the British company expanded its holdings in India. After the first factory on the western coast, came a factory at Madras in 1640, then a trading post in Bombay in 1675, and a fortified one at Calcutta in 1690.

By the middle of the 18th century, with the mighty Mughal empire disintegrating in the hands of effete kings, British merchants began to mix commercial activity with political involvement.

And after the humiliating defeat of the Nawab of Bengal in the Battle of Plassey in 1757, they began assuming direct territorial control over large tracts of the fast-unravelling Mughal empire.

By 1765, the British had managed to convince the no-longer mighty Mughal emperor, a hapless cipher called Shah Alam, to give the 'honourable' Company the *diwani* (the right to collect revenues) of Bengal, Bihar and Orissa 'from generation to generation, for ever and ever'. In an arrangement that set the pattern for much of the British sojourn in India, the Company had power without responsibility – it pocketed the revenues while the local ruler administered and policed the area, without any money to pay his officials or his army.

Slowly but steadily, the British sphere of influence expanded and by 1857, the East India Company had established sway over the subcontinent. That was the summer when much of North India erupted against *Company Bahadur* and paid for its exertions when the British Crown edged out the East India Company to establish its dominion over India.

Smith's Folly in the Qutb Complex, 1829 AD

The change in authority from Company to Crown changed little as far as India was concerned; one form of economic exploitation gave way to another. Under Company rule, it had been the officials who feathered their personal nests; after the Crown took over, it was the British government that reaped the fruits.

A shrewd economic policy ensured that Indian trade suffered and Indian manufacturing was all but destroyed. By the middle of the 19th century, the Indian subcontinent, which only a century earlier had been self-reliant and had a large manufacturing base, was reduced to a backward colony of Britain.

This is not to say that the British rule was a wholly pernicious interlude. Much that was good came out of it. For instance, princely warfare that had become endemic to India after the fall of the Mughals was substantially reduced. And this unity was crystallised by cementing forces like western education, the railways, postage and the electric telegraph.

Darjeeling Himalayan Railway, 1881 AD

But this did not in any way diminish the economic and political discrimination written into colonial rule. Although but one in a series of people who had come seeking the splendours of India, the British had always maintained a stiff distance from the 'natives'. And this got worse after 1857, with the British confining themselves to their Civil Lines and cantonments. Their reserve was reflected in their architecture – an alien composition of Doric columns and gothic arches that did not acknowledge the landscape it was located in.

With the emergence of a national consciousness in the latter half of the 19th century, religions and regions, castes and communities came together in a surge of national self-esteem to oust a power that was bent on maintaining its alienness. And, on the stroke of midnight, 15 August 1947, India came into its own.

The seat of government, New Delhi

QUTB MINAR

Axis of Islam

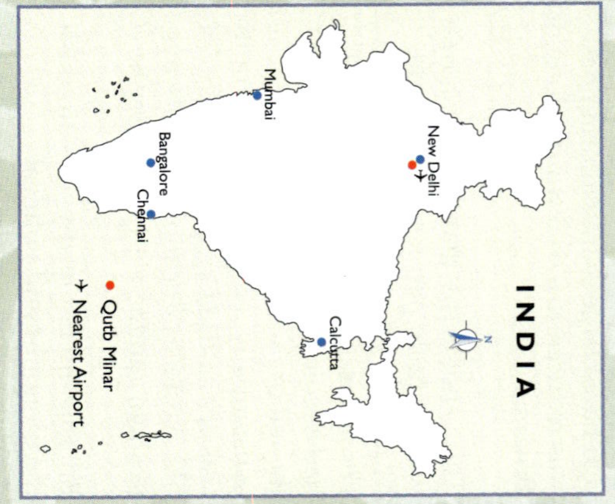

On the southern edge of Delhi, the Qutb Minar spears the sky, marking the site of Delhi's oldest incarnation, Qila Rai Pithora.

The rocky outspur of the Aravalli Ridge around Mehrauli is scattered with ruins dating to the 12th century when the area first passed into Muslim hands. The ramparts of the medieval city built by the Rajput king Prithviraj Chauhan in AD 1180 can still be seen today, although they are intermittently broken by macadamed roads.

Qutb Complex

In AD 1191, the Afghan sultan Mohammed Ghuri led his army south across the Hindu Kush mountains. Fired by their faith, the conquerors swept through the plains destroying Hindu temples and razing Buddhist monasteries. And when, after a year, they reached the arid plains of Delhi, the general who had led the assault, a slave called Qutbuddin Aibak, decided to dedicate Qila Rai Pithora to Islam's victory over the infidel.

1. Alai Darwaza
2. Qutb Minar
3. Quwwatul Islam Masjid
4. Iron Pillar
5. Tomb of Iltutmish
6. Alai Minar
7. Imam Zamin's Tomb

Succeeding Muslim dynasties added to the complex over the next five centuries, making it the cradle of Islamic architecture in India.

The Other Delhis

Delhi has remained the pivot of the North for more than a thousand years. The triangular swathe of land that lay between the Aravalli Hills and the Yamuna was not only fertile, it also commanded the vital trade route from the north-western mountains to the agriculturally abundant Ganga plains.

The area had housed settlements for several millenia, beginning with the mythical Indraprastha, the grand township built by the heroes of the epic *Mahabharata*, the five Pandava brothers. Although there is little archaeological evidence of Indraprastha's existence, local oral tradition strongly perpetrates it. In fact, when the Purana Qila or the Old Fort in Delhi was being cleared of squatters in1911, officials found one of the *bastis* inside the Fort called Indraprata.

The site was continuously inhabited through ancient times, but most of these were village settlements. Archaeological evidence found in Purana Qila and in the Aravalli Hills points to the area being inhabited from 300 BC. However, it is with the beginning of the medieval era that Delhi begins to take on shades of a city.

Towards the end of the first millenium after Christ, a clan of Rajputs called the Tomars rose to prominence in the Aravalli Hills, south of the Delhi area. Their fortress, Lal Kot, was later enlarged by Prithviraj Chauhan, another Rajput ruler who defeated the Tomars.

Quwwatul Islam Masjid

The mosque known as Might of Islam was begun by Qutbuddin Aibak in AD 1192 to celebrate his master, Mohammed Ghuri's victory over the Rajputs and is the oldest surviving mosque in India. When Ghuri was assassinated in 1206, Qutbuddin anointed himself sultan and made the Quwwatul Islam *masjid* the Jami Masjid or the congregational mosque of Delhi.

Passing through the main gateway, you find yourself standing under an intricately carved temple ceiling with richly ornamented pillars on both sides. These were taken from 27 Hindu and Jain temples of Qila Rai Pithora, a fact recorded by Qutbuddin on the main eastern entrance. Some of the pillars with motifs like bells and garlands are still resplendent.

Although the mosque, completed in AD 1198, contains many Arabic architectural features like the use of mud and brick for building and glazed tiles for decoration, it also displays marked Hindu elements. The cloister, for instance, is built entirely of undisguised temple columns, placed rather incongruously one on top of another to achieve the height the Muslim planners wanted.

Left: **The screen of arches at the Quwwatul Islam *masjid*, the oldest surviving mosque in India**

It is this Chauhan citadel called Qila Rai Pithora, which is the first settlement substantial enough to be called a city.

Prithviraj was ousted by the Afghan, Mohammed Ghuri in AD 1192. The Muslim conquerors did not build themselves a new city, but contented themselves with adding mosques and *minars* to Qila Rai Pithora, making it the *qutb* or axis of the sultanate they established here.

A century passed before the first complete Muslim city of Delhi was built by Alauddin Khilji (AD1296-1316). Having repelled Mongol raiders, Alauddin walled his camp just north of Qila Rai Pithora and peopled it. Local legend, in fact, traces the name Siri to the 8,000 heads – the Hindustani word for 'head' is *sir* – of defeated Mongols that were supposedly embedded in the city walls!

Ghiyasuddin Tughlaq (1320-25), the founder of the dynasty that followed the Khiljis had grander plans for his capital. He selected a site some 8 kms east of Siri for his walled city. Within four years, Tughlaqabad was ready – all laid out in neat grids. However, after Ghiyasuddin's death, his city was abandoned largely due to the lack of drinking water. Legend, of course, tells it differently. Ghiyasuddin, it is said, had a less than sunny relationship with the resident saint of Delhi, Nizamuddin Auliya. And relations soured further when the ruler pressed those very masons building the *baoli* or water tank at the saint's *dargah*, for work on his own city.

The sandstone screen at the western end of the courtyard, too, has carved lotuses mingling with Koranic calligraphy in happy fusion. The screen is a series of arches in the corbelling style favoured by the Hindu craftsmen who built it.

Quwwatul Islam mosque was enlarged in AD 1230. Qutbuddin's successor and son-in-law, Iltutmish, doubled the size of the mosque by extending its colonnades and prayer-hall to accommodate the increasing numbers of the faithful.

Alauddin Khilji of the next dynasty to rule Delhi again enlarged the enclosure in the first quarter of the 14th century and also added gateways on the eastern, northern and southern walls.

Below:
The cloister of the Quwwatul Islam mosque is built of undisguised temple pillars. The mosque was raised by Qutbuddin Aibak using the remains of 27 Hindu and Jain temples destroyed by his over-zealous army.

Above:
Hindu floral motifs interspersed with Islamic calligraphy on the Qutb Minar

The workmen obeyed the royal decree but continued to work for Nizamuddin at night. Upon which, an enraged king forbade the sale of oil that lit their lamps. Nizamuddin apparently worked a miracle and the water of the freshly-dug tank turned to oil. And to round off, cursed Ghiyasuddin's new city, *Ya rahe Gujjar/ Ya rahe ujjar* ('May it be inhabited by herdsmen/ Or else remain desolate').

Whatever the cause of Tughlaqabad's demise, Ghiyasuddin's successor Mohammed bin Tughlaq returned to the original Rajput site. However, the Mongols threatened again, and the new ruler decided to wall Qila Rai Pithora, Siri and the suburbs between them to build his Jahanpanah or Refuge of the World.

The last Tughlaq of note, Firoz Shah Tughlaq (1351-88) also built his own city, Firozabad, further north along the Yamuna. And though it ceased to be an administrative centre after his death, Firozabad remained peopled right until the 18th century.

Succeeding dynasties were so occupied with keeping their realms intact that they had little time to spare for city building. The second Mughal emperor, Humayun started building a city he called Dinpanah or Refuge of Religion in 1533, using a brick from Siri as its founding stone. But Humayun soon lost his empire to Sher Shah Suri (1540-45). The Afghan general took over not only the Mughal's empire but also his city project.

Qutb Minar

Soaring high above the Quwwatul Islam mosque is the tower Sultan Qutbuddin Aibak built in AD 1199 to celebrate the invincibility of Islam. Although modelled as a classical *minar* or tower from which the *muezzin* calls the faithful to prayers, the Qutb Minar was a symbolic rather than a functional structure. It would be an extraordinary *muezzin* who would expect to be heard from a height of 72.5 metres – assuming, in the first place, that he managed to trudge up the 379 steps five times each day, every day.

The Minar was a symbol of the military might of the Turko-Afghan Slave dynasty – so called because its earliest kings were all slaves of their predecessors – and the *qutb* or axis of Islamic dominion. An inscription on the tower says that it was erected by Qutbuddin, literally Staff of God, to 'cast the shadow of God over both East and West'.

Qutbuddin lived to see only the first storey finished, and it was his successor Iltutmish who completed the next two floors. According to some Nagari and Persian inscriptions on the tower, the Qutb Minar was damaged twice by lightning.

Known as Shergarh or the Lair of the Tiger, this city along the river bank, south of Firozabad, is the site today known as Purana Qila.

Humayun retrieved his empire from Sher Shah in 1555 but died a year later. His son Akbar took his court off to Agra and then to Fatehpur Sikri. In 1639, Akbar's grandson Shahjahan returned to Delhi from Agra and began building a new city. Architects and astrologers were summoned to oversee the building of the new capital of an empire that had ruled unbroken for over a century. Imperial Shahjahanabad was suitably impressive. It had a citadel, Lal Qila or Red Fort, royal residences, mosques, wide streets and teeming bazaars – all within a wall pierced by 14 gates.

Delhi remained the axis of the Mughal empire until the 1857 Uprising when the British, based at Calcutta, unseated the then emperor. It returned to importance in 1911 when King George V, on an imperial visit to India, announced that Delhi would be reinstated First City.

Edwin Lutyens, the man behind many of England's stately homes, was summoned. He teamed up with Herbert Baker, who had done a spot of colonial city-building in Pretoria, to build the new Delhi. The city they built was suitably imperial – imposing official buildings, wide roads and elegant bungalows, all set in a sea of green.

And when the empire retreated, it bequeathed New Delhi to a new nation.

In AD 1368, a bolt knocked off the top floor and the then sultan, Firoz Shah Tughlaq, restored it, adding two floors and introducing white marble to the exterior of an otherwise red and buff sandstone structure.

The circular tower with its pronounced taper that increases the illusion of height, has a base diameter of 14.3 metres, while the top floor measures 2.7 metres in diameter. The inner staircase has been closed since 1979 when a party of schoolgirls panicked when the lights failed. Several students were killed in the stampede.

The first three storeys of Qutb Minar are indented with heavily carved flutings. The pattern of the flutings is different on each of the three floors. It is alternately round and angular on the bottom storey, round on the second and angular on the third.

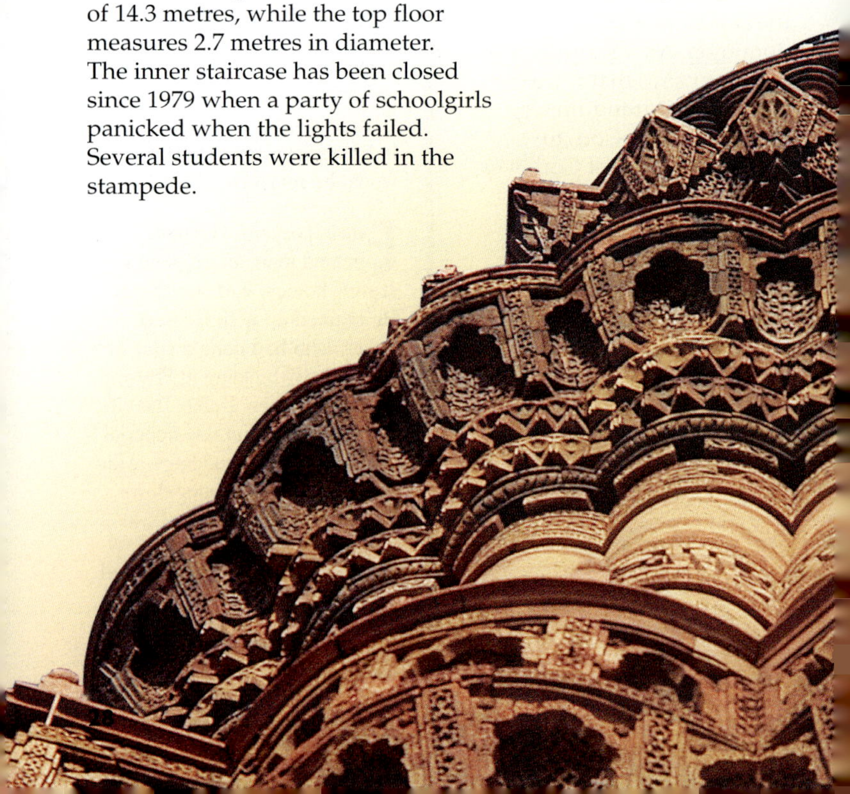

The Qutb Minar has survived a series of tremors in the eight centuries it has towered over Delhi, acquiring a slight tilt that leaves it some two feet off the perpendicular.

An earthquake in the early 19th century destroyed its crowning cupola. An English engineer, Major Robert Smith, replaced it in 1829, but his addition looked so grossly out of place that it was removed in 1848 by Governor-General Lord Hardinge. It now stands on the lawns and has acquired the sobriquet Smith's Folly.

Till a while ago, the base of the Minar had a number of glass plates banded by concrete, installed by the Archaeological Survey of India to monitor earthquakes.

Smith's Folly

Each balcony of the Qutb Minar is supported on a web of tiny arches, a Persian technique termed *muqarnas*

The arch of the Quwwatul Islam mosque

The Hindu temples of North India seldom featured arches. The gateways of these temples were either flat-roofed or else modelled on mountain peaks, with the layers of stones increasing in length until they met in a peak above two pillars.

Muslim Sultans wanted to recreate the pointed arches that had fired the imagination of Islamic architects ever since they were first built in the mosque of Samarra in Iraq, in AD 752.

But the local masons were unfamiliar with the keystone technique that held up an arch. This involved arranging and cutting individual wedge-shaped stones in such a manner that they formed a semi-circle whose centre was also the centre of the arch. The centre stone of the arch was called the keystone and carried the weight of the arch.

Pressed by their Muslim masters, Hindu craftsmen innovated the corbelled arch. They laid their stones horizontally and in layers of increasing length like they had done for their peaked gateways.

But they rounded the sides of individual stones to form the curved lines of an arch. This was also called the sham arch and is the style seen in the Quwwatul Islam mosque.

Iron Pillar

In the courtyard of the Quwwatul Mosque stands an Iron Pillar bearing a Sanskrit inscription in the style of the fourth century Gupta rulers. The writing indicates that the pillar was probably a *dhvajastambha* or flagpole of a 4th-5th century Vishnu temple, wrought, most likely, at the behest of Chandragupta II who ruled between AD 375 and 413.

No one really knows how the Iron Pillar got here but what is remarkable about this 7 metre-high pillar is that it has remained completely rust free for over 1,500 years.

FESTIVALS

- **Phoolwalon Ki Sair** (Flower Sellers' Walk): This festival unique to Mehrauli is celebrated in September every year.
- **Qutb Festival**

An annual festival of classical music and dance is held in October within the Qutb Complex.

Tomb of Iltutmish

In AD 1235, Sultan Iltutmish built himself a tomb just outside the extension he had added to the Quwwatul Islam *masjid*.

The tomb itself is rather plain on the outside, but the interior is covered with inscriptions from the *Koran* which have been so delicately carved that they seem like lacework in stone.

Alai Minar

The gigantic structure of rubble to the north of Qutb Minar is the 25.5 metre-high unfinished base of a mammoth tower Alauddin Khilji had planned as a rival to the Qutb Minar when he returned in triumph from his Deccan campaign. However, the Sultan died before even the first storey was finished and the project was abandoned.

Tomb of Iltutmish: The dome of the monument has not survived

COURTESY: THE GOLDEN CALM, M.M. KAYE, VIKING PRESS, NEW YORK, 1980

Alai Darwaza

By the time Alauddin Khilji began building the southern gateway to the Quwwatul Islam mosque in AD 1311, the Indian workmen had mastered the art of constructing the dome using squinches, or arches set diagonally across the corners of a square chamber to turn it into an octagon, before topping the structure with a dome.

The Alai Darwaza, built of red sandstone, is 17.2 metres square and has arched openings on all sides. The northern arch is semi-circular, while the other three are shaped, in the classic Islamic style, like pointed horseshoes. The gateway also displays other Muslim architectural elements like the central knob on the dome and the lotus buds that fringe each arch.

The interior of the gateway is profusely carved with geometric symbols and inscriptions in the Naqsh script. The decorations in red stone, interspersed with the inscriptional bands in white marble make for a very pleasing prospect.

Alai Darwaza:
The gateway to Quwwatul Islam mosque, added by Sultan Alauddin Khilji in 1311, is a fine example of early Islamic architecture. It is perhaps the earliest building in the subcontinent to feature the now typical knob on the dome

Tomb of Imam Zamin

Step out through the eastern door of the Alai Darwaza to reach the octagonal tomb of Imam Mohammed Ali, a Turkish holy man who came to India in the reign of Sikandar Lodi (AD 1488-1517) and was revered as Imam Zamin.

Left:
The use of red sandstone and white marble which was to become a favourite device of Mughal builders appears for the first time in Alai Darwaza

Below:
Just outside the Qutb Complex, is the octagonal tomb of Adham Khan built in 1562, locally known as Bhulbhulaiyan or labyrinth

COURTESY: THE GOLDEN CALM, VIKING PRESS, NEW YORK, 1980

GETTING THERE

By Air:
Delhi's Indira Gandhi International Airport is 14 kms away.

By Rail:
- New Delhi Railway Station (16 kms)
- Hazrat Nizamuddin Railway Station (14 kms)
- Old Delhi Railway Station (18 kms)

By Road:
The Qutb is 14 kms from the city centre at Connaught Place

HUMAYUN'S TOMB

A Grand Memorial

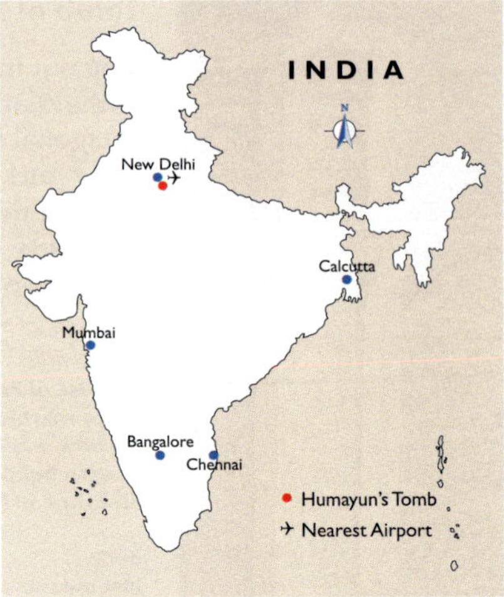

Babur, a prince descended from Genghis Khan and Timur, established the Mughal dynasty in India. He was succeeded in AD 1530 by his son Humayun, an engaging but irresolute monarch who temporarily lost control of the empire and so nearly ended the Mughal dynasty almost as soon as it had begun. In 1540, the Muslim ruler of Bihar and Bengal, Sher Shah Suri, dislodged him from the Delhi throne. This interregnum was brought to an end in AD 1555 when Humayun regained control.

During the ten years of his rule Humayun was continuously engaged in warfare with little leisure for intellectual or cultural pursuits, including architecture.

Humayun's Tomb

COURTESY: THE GOLDEN CALM BY M.M.KAYE, VIKING PRESS, NEW YORK, I

However, in AD 1538 he laid the foundations of a new city, Dinpanah or the Refuge of the Faithful, on the bank of the Yamuna in Delhi. It was completed in just ten months with massive walls, bastions and gates.

But no trace of it now remains, as it was pulled down systematically by Sher Shah Suri.

The inner citadel of this city is today known as Purana Qila or Old Fort. Within six years, Humayun was ousted by Sher Shah Suri who promptly renamed the city Shergarh. After regaining his throne, Humayun is said to have completed parts of the Purana Qila left unfinished by Sher Shah.

The Mughals

In April 1526, with the sun gathering heat, a Muslim chief swept into India from the north. There was nothing new in this – for several centuries now, Muslim chiefs had ridden down the Hindu Kush mountains to raid or rule the subcontinent.

It was with a relatively small force, but one armed with artillery, that Babur, the prince from Farghana, defeated Ibrahim Lodi, the then ruler of Delhi, at the Battle of Panipat in 1526.

The dynasty Babur founded was named Mughal, a distorted reference to their Mongol ancestry. Although it was the sixth Muslim house to rule Delhi in three centuries, it was the only one which bred emperors.

Over the next five generations, the Mughals dotted the landscape of northern India with beautiful monuments – there are palaces and forts, mosques and mausoleums, and even whole cities.

The first Mughal emperor, Babur, did not have the time or perhaps the inclination to indulge in building projects. His son Humayun did try and build himself an imperial city on the banks of the Yamuna in Delhi. However, he lost both his kingdom and his city to a general from the east, Sher Shah Suri.

It was ironically a woman who set the tone for Mughal architecture. Humayun's widow, the dowager empress Haji Begum brought in a Persian architect to build her husband's tomb.

Humayun died soon after regaining the throne of Delhi in AD 1555. He was climbing down the stairs of the Sher Mandal, a two-storeyed pavilion in Purana Qila believed to have been used as a library by him, when he heard the call of the *muezzin* for prayer and slipped in his haste. He never recovered from the fall and died in 1556.

A miniature painting of the reclusive Humayun

Unlike most Muslim rulers and dignitaries in India, Humayun had not built his own tomb. It was some years before he was finally laid to rest in a tomb to the south of the Purana Qila, near the shrine of Sheikh Nizamuddin Auliya, which even today attracts a constant throng of devotees.

Humayun's Tomb inaugurates a sequence of grand Mughal burial chambers. The Taj Mahal is known to have been inspired by Humayun's Tomb, and in many ways this magnificent red and white building is as spectacular as the famous 'monument to love' in Agra. Humayun's Tomb was commissioned in 1560 by his senior widow, known as Haji Begum, who is said to have spent one and a half million rupees on the building.

The marble dome of Humayun's Tomb is the first full dome in Mughal architecture; all earlier ones were half domes

This building inaugurates a sequence of grand Mughal mausolea, culminating in that requiem in marble, the Taj Mahal. Although Islamic tenets dictate that a Muslim's grave be covered only by earth and be open to air, the Mughals turned mausoleum-making into an overwhelming art.

Humayun's son, Akbar, consolidated the Mughal empire, and also made patronage of the arts and architecture a royal obligation. Poetry, painting and music flourished in his reign, as did architecture. He gave his empire a fulcrum in the fort at Agra, then gave himself a new city at Fatehpur Sikri and, in between, he built numerous mosques, *dargahs* and commemorative buildings.

Abul Fazl, the royal chronicler notes the political advantage of Akbar's propensity for building: 'Mighty fortresses have been raised, which protect the timid, frighten the rebellious and please the obedient'.

His son Jahangir, was fond of laying elaborate gardens in the Persian manner and had several created in Lahore and Kashmir. However, Jahangir was an indifferent builder and the one major monument he built, his father Akbar's tomb at Sikandra reflects this.

In fact, the tomb that Jahangir's favourite queen, Noor Jahan, built for her father at Agra, is a far superior monument. A gem-like building, the tomb of Itmad-ud-daula is faced with white marble and covered entirely with *pietra dura*.

The splendour of this monument becomes evident on entering the huge double-storeyed gateway. High rubble walls enclose a square garden divided into four large squares separated by causeways and water channels.

Each square is divided again into smaller squares by pathways, forming a typical Mughal garden called *charbagh*. The fountains were worked with simple yet highly-developed engineering skills quite common in India during this period.

During the Uprising of 1857, Humayun's Tomb was the scene of the demise of the Mughal dynasty. The last emperor, Bahadur Shah II, sought sanctuary in the tomb of his ancestor when the Uprising collapsed, before he was arrested by the British.

The garden is laid out in the classical grid of the *charbagh*

The lofty mausoleum is located at the centre of the enclosure and rises from a platform faced with a series of cells with arched openings. Inside, the tomb consists of an octagonal hall that rises through two storeys, and is surrounded by smaller octagonal chambers.

The main sarcophagus stands in the central hall, oriented – in accordance with Muslim practice – on the north-south axis. Traditionally, the body is placed with the head to the north, the face turned sideways towards Mecca.

Akbar inspecting the building work of Fatehpur Sikri – illustration from the *Akbarnama*

The fourth Mughal emperor, Shahjahan was perhaps the greatest builder. The Mughal fusion style of architecture reached its maturity with Shahjahan. Although the Mughals were foreign invaders, they did not impose an alien architecture on the Indian landscape.

While they imported ideas from Persia, the Mughals were forced to depend upon local, largely Hindu, craftsmen to do the actual work. These artisans had a thousand-year-old architectural tradition of their own. So there are hundreds of Mughal monuments which are conceived in the classical Islamic style, complete with minarets and pointed arches, but also sport the *chhatris*, *chhajjas* and *jalis* beloved by Hindu builders and decorated with organic rather than just geometric motifs.

Each side is dominated by three lofty arches, the central one being the highest. This plan is repeated on the second storey, and the roof is surmounted by a 42.5 metre-high double dome of marble with pillared kiosks or *chhatris* placed around it. The dome is what is called a full dome, a complete semi-circle. All Mughal domes were full domes, all previous domes half-domes, or only half semi-circles. On the top of the dome there is a crescent, but no lotus as the architect was a Persian. The structure is built with red sandstone, but white and black marble has been used in the borders to relieve the monotony.

Left:
The prominent *iwan* or central arch of Humayun's Tomb

Below:
The *jali* or trellis screen, used to perfection under Shahjahan, makes its first appearance in Humayun's Tomb

The general effect of the central hall is now a little spartan, but originally it was softened by furnishings. The English merchant William Finch visited the building in AD 1611 and described it as 'spread with rich carpets, the tombe itself covered with a pure white sheet, a rich semiane (coloured tent) over head, and in front certaine bookes on small tressels, by which stand his sword, tucke (turban) and shooes'.

Within the compound of Humayun's Tomb are many small monuments: To the southeast stands an impressive square tomb with a double-dome. Usually referred to as **Nai ka Gumbad** or the Barber's Tomb, it is said to have been built for the Emperor's favourite barber. It is interesting to note that barbers seem to play a prominent part in the lives of Delhi rulers. Mohammed bin Tughlaq's barber was given his own fort, Nai ka Kot or Barber's Fort, near Adilabad.

GETTING THERE

By Air:
Indira Gandhi International Airport (Domestic Terminal) is 17 kms away

By Rail:
- New Delhi Railway Station (8 kms)
- Hazrat Nizamuddin Railway Station (1 km)
- Old Delhi Railway Station (12 kms)

By Road:
The tomb is 5 kms from city centre at Connaught Place

Entry fee: Rs 5
Free on Fridays

South of the main pathway leading to Humayun's Tomb is a picturesque gateway which leads to a walled enclosure called **Arab ki Sarai**. This was built by Humayun's widow for the 300 Arab merchants she is said to have brought with her from a pilgrimage to Mecca.

Within the eastern enclosure of the Arab ki Sarai is **Afsarwala Tomb and Masjid**.

Further west on the main pathway is the gateway to the now, rather barren **Bu Halima's garden**. Nothing much is known of this lady; the gateway and two very ornamental *chhattris* are all that remain of the garden.

On the south-west end of Bu Halima's garden is the octagonal **Tomb of Isa Khan**, a nobleman in the court of Sher Shah.

Tomb of Khan-i-Khanan: Just outside Humayun's Tomb is the tomb of Abdur Rahim Khan who assumed the title of Khan-i-Khanan (died1625). The now dilapidated tomb was an architectural landmark in its time, since it followed the design of Humayun's Tomb and had a marble dome.

Humayun's Tomb stands on a eight metre-high platform

AGRA FORT

Mighty Mughal Citadel

The high, red sandstone walls loom over the Yamuna river. Behind this row of battlements and bastions lies a refined world of marble pavilions, landscaped gardens and serene mosques. The Fort in Agra, in the northern Indian state of Uttar Pradesh, is one of earliest surviving Mughal buildings in the city. Babur is said to have laid out gardens here but no sign of them remains.

The history of Agra as an imperial city begins with Akbar. His predecessors, Babur and Humayun never got the opportunity to plan any grand buildings. It was Akbar who laid the foundation of the empire and then built this majestic citadel to match his achievements. With the new Fort, Agra got a new name – Akbarabad.

Khas Mahal

The site was chosen because the river here acted as a natural moat. An older brick fort built by the Lodi sultans that stood at the site was demolished and, according to the *Akbarnama*, some 3,000 to 4,000 'skilled masons, hardy labourers and other staff' toiled daily to raise the first-ever fort enclosed by stone walls. The red sandstone walls rose to a height of 22 metres and stretched a distance of over a kilometre.

This Mughal miniature painting gives a bird's-eye view of Agra Fort

Akbar's son, Jahangir, notes in his memoirs that Agra Fort and the buildings within it cost the royal exchequer a tidy Rs 3.5 million.

The walls of Agra Fort conceal a pleasing world of palaces and pavilions

On the city side, there was a deep moat between two layers of high, protective battlements. The Fort was built in a crescent shape following the curve of the river and the walls were pierced by slits to allow musketeers to fire at the enemy. Drawbridges over the moat led to four giant gateways. Two of the gates, the Hathi Pol and the Amar Singh Gate, with Naqqar Khanas or Drum Houses built over them, are still in use.

Agra Fort established the model for all Mughal forts that followed. Akbar himself built forts at Lahore, Allahabad and Fatehpur Sikri.

His grandson, Shahjahan, an even greater builder, built the Red Fort, the citadel in his new capital city of Shahjahanabad, with the same layout.

1. Ticket Office
2. Jahangiri Mahal
3. Jodhabai's Palace
4. Golden Pavillions
5. Khas Mahal
6. Anguri Bagh
7. Mussaman Burj
8. Sheesh Mahal
9. Diwan-i-Khas
10. Black Marble Throne
11. Machhi Bhavan
12. Nagina Masjid
13. Diwan-i-Am
14. Moti Masjid

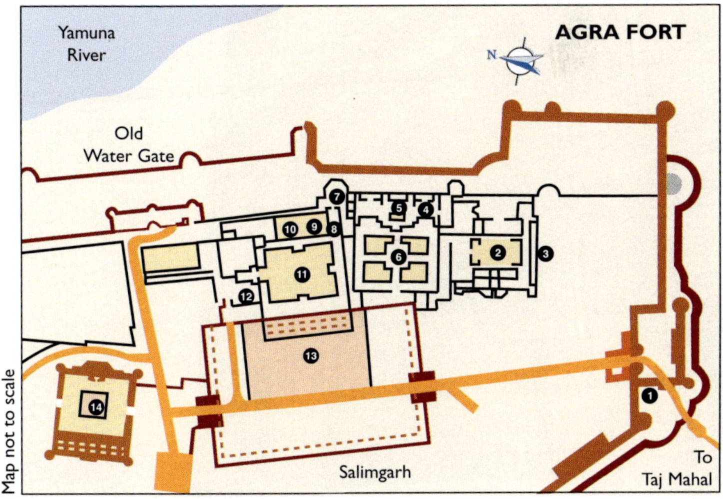

'He gave directions for the building in Agra – which by its position in the centre of Hindustan – of a grand fortress such as might be worthy thereof, and correspond to the dignity of his dominions….'

– Royal chronicler Abul Fazl writing about Akbar's decision to build a new citadel in 1565

Abul Fazl mentions over five hundred buildings within the Fort. However, apart from the walls and the gateways, few of the Akbari structures survive today. Shahjahan demolished many of the sandstone buildings, remodelled others and built his own marble palaces.

The Fort faced more destruction during the twilight years of the Mughal empire when the marauding Jats took away the marble and *pietra dura* pillars for their own palaces. The final assault came from the British who sent off the royal baths to London to be exhibited in palaces and destroyed many other buildings, replacing them with ugly army barracks.

But enough remains to give the visitor a flavour of the past. What makes it more interesting is the fact that one can trace here the architectural styles of the three emperors who ruled from the Agra Fort.

Akbar's imposing citadel was planned as a statement of imperial power

Enter Agra Fort from the soaring portal of the Amar Singh Gate to the south, and turn right to see the only surviving palace built by Akbar. **Jahangiri Mahal** is said to have been built somewhere around AD 1570 by Akbar for his son Salim, who later took the title of Jahangir. Some scholars feel that the palace could not have been named Jahangiri Mahal during Akbar's lifetime, as his son was then known as Salim. Also, the layout, with its rooms opening onto an inner courtyard, is more on the lines of a harem.

Entry Fee:
Rs 15 for Indians and Rs 50 for foreigners. Children below 12 years free.

Free entry on Fridays

Best season:
October to March.

The red sandstone Jahangiri Mahal is the first example of Akbar's attempt to blend ornate Hindu motifs with the more symmetrical Islamic style. The outer walls of the Jahangiri Mahal have a facade of carved blind arches highlighted in marble. The rooms surround an inner courtyard with halls to the north and south.

A colonial artist's rendering of Agra Fort

Stone *jalis* screen the passageways that were used by the women of the household. There is also an open porch that overlooks the river. The rooms have finely-carved columns and niches and the palace may have been used by Jahangir's powerful queen Noor Jahan.

The rest of the monuments in Agra Fort are built by Shahjahan and from robust sandstone we move to the era of lustrous marble. In 1636 Shahjahan built his luxurious personal palace, **Khas Mahal.** He also added two flanking pavilions topped with the curved *bangaldar* roofs – so termed because the shape recalled village huts of Bengal – and had the **Anguri Bagh** garden laid out in front. The airy palace with delicate arches, fountains and tapering turrets overlooks the river. The walls and pillars once had exquisite inlay in semi-precious stones.

In his last years when Shahjahan was imprisoned in the Fort by his son Aurangzeb, he was accompanied by his elder daughter Jahanara who lived in the Khas Mahal.

Khas Mahal flanked by smaller pavilions with curved *bangaldar* roofs

The Anguri Bagh, or Garden of Grapes, has no vines but geometric flower beds, water channels and fountains in the traditional *charbagh* style.

At the north-east corner of the Anguri Bagh is the **Mussaman Burj** or the Octagonal Tower, also known as Jasmine Tower. Crowned with a copper dome, this tower placed on a bastion provides a panoramic view of the river.

It is an exquisite little building which is supposed to have been Mumtaz Mahal's private quarters and has all the elegant appurtenances fit for a queen – from walls and columns covered with delicate *pietra dura*, a sculpted ornamental pool in the floor, *jali* screens and rows of carved niches to hold the queen's personal effects.

Left:
Khas Mahal:
This serene pavilion with its painted ceiling was probably one of Emperor Shahjahan's private palaces

Peacock Throne

The extraordinary seat of Shahjahan's empire was a wonder of wealth. It comprised an enamelled canopy studded with gems. Its underside was inlaid with diamonds, emeralds, rubies and garnets and it was supported by 12 pillars covered with emerald facing. It got its name from the jewelled peacocks that flanked it.

Shahjahan's official biographer noted the commissioning of the throne in 1634 saying, 'In the course of years, many valuable gems had come into the imperial jewel-house, each one of which might serve as an ear-drop for Venus, or would adorn the girdle of the Sun. Upon the accession of the emperor, it occurred to his mind that...the acquisition of such rare jewels...can only render one service, that of adorning the throne of empire'.

When Shahjahan moved court to Delhi, he took his showy throne with him and when the rapacious Nadir Shah tore into the city in 1739, he carted it off to Persia.

Steps lead up from the Mussaman Burj to the **Diwan-i-Khas** or the Hall of Private Audience, where important matters of state were conducted. Completed in 1637, the open hall has lavishly carved marble columns and arches with inlay work as well as carvings in relief. At the other end of its terrace are two thrones, one in white marble and the other in black, which was the one Jahangir used.

The terrace overlooks a courtyard quaintly named **Machhi Bhavan**, or the Palace of Fishes, which points to the garden in front of it once containing ornamental fish ponds. This courtyard was where the court's ladies held their special *bazaars* and festivals.

To the west of Machhi Bhavan, steps lead down to the red sandstone **Diwan-i-Am**, the Hall of Public Audience, which is the template for the one in Delhi's Red Fort. It is a superbly proportioned, colonnaded building with three-rows of cusped arches supported by slender pillars. There is a high decorated recess in the rear wall which was where Shahjahan sat in state on the bejewelled Peacock Throne, dealing with administrative

GETTING THERE

Air:
Kheria Airport is 7 kms from centre of town. Delhi, 204 kms away, has an international airport

By Rail:
The Agra Cantonment station is the nearest railhead

By Road:
UP Roadways' buses leave for other major cities from the Idgah bus stand

Timing: 7 am to 6 pm

Entry Fee:
Rs 15 for Indians and Rs 50 for foreigners. Children below 12 years free.

Free entry on Fridays

Best time to visit:
October to March.

Moti Masjid: This serene mosque is remarkable for the purity of its architecture

matters, making pronouncements, hearing petitions and dispensing justice.

There are three mosques within the Fort. **Nagina Masjid** has three graceful domes and was used by the women of the harem. Then, there is the tiny **Mina Masjid**, located near the Mussaman Burj which is now closed to the public. The third is the **Moti Masjid** or the Pearl Mosque, which was built by Shahjahan for his personal use.

The pillared hall, Diwan-i-Am, with its cusped arches became Shahjahan's architectural signature

TAJ MAHAL

Requiem in Marble

For centuries, the Taj Mahal has inspired poets, painters and musicians to try and capture its elusive magic in word, colour and song. It is one of the most flawless architectural creations of the world. Since the 17th century, travellers have crossed continents to come and see this ultimate memorial to love, and few have been unmoved by its incomparable beauty.

Taj Mahal stands in the city of Agra, in the northern Indian state of Uttar Pradesh, on the banks of the Yamuna river. It was built in the memory of the beautiful Arjumand Bano Begum, who won the heart of a Mughal prince. She was married at 21 to Emperor Jahangir's third son Prince Khurram and stayed loyally by his side through good times and bad: in the luxurious royal palaces of Agra as well as the transient tents of war camps.

Taj Mahal

Emperor Shahjahan was a passionate builder and visualised the Taj Mahal, picking out the best elements from designs offered by several architects. His buildings always had the stamp of his sense of aesthetic.

In AD 1628, Khurram became king after a bloody battle of succession; he took the name Shahjahan or King of the World and showered his beloved *begum* with the highest titles. She became Mumtaz Mahal, the Exalted of the Palace and Mumtaz-ul-Zamani, the Exalted of the Age. But Mumtaz Mahal was not destined to be queen for long.

In 1631, Shahjahan went on an expedition to the South and, as always, Mumtaz Mahal accompanied him. But she died in childbirth at Burhanpur. She had borne Shahjahan fourteen children, of whom four sons and three daughters survived. When Mumtaz Mahal died, she was just 39 years old. Shahjahan was inconsolable and contemporary chronicles tell of the royal court mourning for two years. There was no music, no feasting, and no celebration of any kind.

Shahjahan, who was a passionate builder, now decided to erect a memorial to his queen in pristine

marble that the world would never forget. The site selected for the tomb was a garden by the Yamuna river, unshadowed by any other structure. The garden had been laid by Raja Man Singh of Amber and now belonged to his grandson, Raja Jai Singh. By a royal *firman*, Shahjahan gave Jai Singh four *havelis* in exchange for the garden. The site was also chosen because it was located on a bend in the river, and so could be seen from Shahjahan's personal palace in Agra Fort, further upstream.

Work on the mausoleum began in 1633 and 20,000 workers laboured for 17 years to build it. The most skilled architects, inlay craftsmen, calligraphers, stone-carvers and masons came from all across India and lands as distant as Persia and Turkey. The master mason was from Baghdad, an expert in building the double dome from Persia, and an inlay specialist from Delhi.

Who designed Taj Mahal?

That question has never been answered. Countries from Persia and Turkey to France and Italy have claimed credit. The chronicles of the time mention only one Ustad Ahmed Lahori as the *Mimar-i-kul* or chief architect. But this was, traditionally, merely a supervisory post. An inscription on Lahori's grave at Aurangabad says that he was the builder of Taj Mahal and the Jami Masjid in Delhi.

Taj Mahal is ultimately the culmination of two centuries of evolving designs of Mughal tombs, beginning with Humayun's Tomb in Delhi.

Timing:
8 am to 7 pm.
Closed Mondays

Entrance Fee:
Rs 15 for the Taj Mahal and the Museum from 10 am-5 pm

Rs 100 from 8 am–10 am and 5 pm – 7 pm. Children below 12 free.

Free on Fridays.

Foreigners are charged a composite fee of Rs 500 that allows them entry to all the monuments in Agra: Taj Mahal, Agra Fort, Itmad-ud-Daula and Sikandra

Best time to visit:
October to March

The tomb was completed in AD 1650. But, Shahjahan was deposed by his son Aurangzeb in 1658 and imprisoned in the Agra Fort. He spent his last years in the Mussaman Burj looking downstream at the Taj where his beloved Mumtaz Mahal lay. Sixteen years later he, too, was laid to rest beside her.

Shahjahan's two biggest passions were architecture and jewellery and both are reflected in the Taj Mahal. He visualised a building in marble and then had it decorated with semi-precious stones inlaid with the delicacy of handcrafted jewellery. Marble in purest white was brought from Makrana in Rajasthan, yellow marble and rockspar from the banks of the Narmada river, black marble from Charkoh and red sandstone from Sikri. For the intricate *pietra dura* the finest gems were collected – crystal and jade from China, lapis lazuli and sapphires from Sri Lanka, jasper from Punjab, carnelian from Baghdad and turquoise from Tibet.

Right:
Plan and section of Taj Mahal: The monument has been designed with great precision. The height of the tomb without its finial and including the platform is equal to each side of its plan perimeter. Thus, the Taj forms a perfect cube.

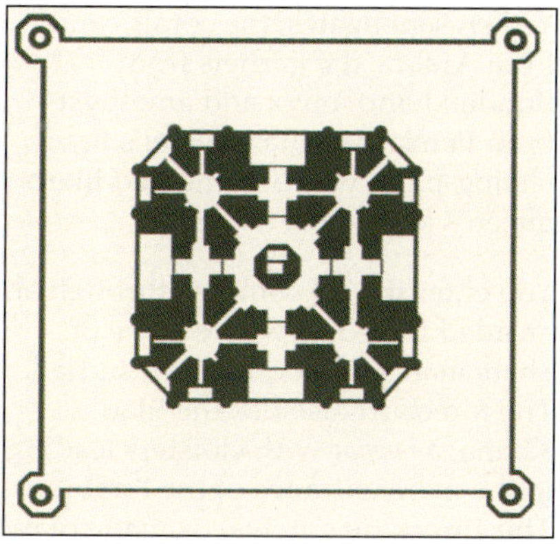

The Taj stands in a landscaped Mughal garden, flanked by two identical buildings in sandstone that set off its pristine marble to stunning effect

Yemen sent agates, the corals came from Arabia, the garnets from Bundelkhand, onyx and amethyst from Persia. Mumtaz Mahal's final resting-place was ornamented like a queen's jewel-box.

Relief carvings on Taj Mahal

You enter the Taj complex through an arcaded forecourt where some of Shahjahan's other queens lie buried. The forecourt also has the Jilau Khana, a *bazaar* with cloisters leading to the main entrance of the tomb. This imposing gateway is made of red sandstone highlighted with marble and has octagonal kiosks on top. The gateway is an imposing 30 metres high and a fitting entrance to the Taj Mahal. The soaring arch is inscribed with a beautiful design of inlaid flowers and calligraphy.

As you enter the dark octagonal chamber under the gateway, the light streaming in from the opposite doorway draws you towards it. Here, framed by the arch of the doorway, the Taj Mahal reveals itself to the viewer with dramatic power. It stands at the end of a long walkway, framed by landscaped gardens and an ever-changing sky, its snowy marble glittering in the sunlight.

Local women placing flowers on the tombs of Mumtaz Mahal and Shahjahan

Taj Mahal stands at one side of a garden laid in the traditional *charbagh* style, with its square lawns bisected by pathways, water channels and rows of fountains. Halfway down the path there is a square pool, its limpid waters reflecting the marble tomb. Unlike other tombs, Taj Mahal stands at one end of the garden instead of the centre. This was done deliberately, to leave its vista uncluttered by any other building.

The ornate *pietra dura* is balanced by carvings in relief to create a sense of harmony

The tomb stands on a marble plinth six-metres high. The four minarets at each corner beautifully frame the tomb. The plinth stands on a high sandstone platform and at the far ends of this base are two identical sandstone structures, a mosque to the west and its *jawab*, or echo, to the east. This was the *mehman khana* or guesthouse. Thus, the main building is not just of great size but beautifully proportioned and balanced in design.

The octagonal central hall has four smaller octagonal halls around it and is decorated with magnificent inlay and dado panels done in high relief. The bulbous, perfectly-balanced double dome rises to a height of 45 metres and the four *chhattris* flanking and balancing the high drum give it added height. Taj Mahal rises 75 metres high and is, in fact, taller than the Qutb Minar.

An ornate marble screen, carved so fine that it almost has the texture of lace surrounds the cenotaphs in the central hall. However, as was the tradition during Mughal times, the actual graves lie in an underground crypt directly below the cenotaphs.

GETTING THERE

By Air:
Kheria Airport is 7 kms from the city centre. Delhi's Indira Gandhi International Airport is 204 kms away.

By Rail:
The nearest railhead for the Taj Mahal is Agra Cantonement railway station, 6 kms from the city centre.

By Road:
Uttar Pradesh State Road Transport Corporation buses leave for other cities from the Idgah bus stand.

What is most amazing about Taj Mahal is the fine detailing. The coloured inlay is never allowed to overwhelm the design, as carvings done in relief sensitively balance it. The ornate *pietra dura* and relief carvings are of floral, calligraphic and geometric designs. However, flowers remain the main decorative element as the tomb depicts a paradise garden. The skill of the inlay worker is so fine that it is impossible to find the joints, even when as many as 40 tiny pieces of semi-precious stones have been used in the petals of a single flower. Some of the best calligraphy of Koranic verses can be seen around the entrance arches and on the two headstones.

Taj Mahal changes its moods with the seasons and the different times of the day. At dawn, the marble has a delicate bloom in shell pink, by noon it glitters majestically white, turning to a soft pearly grey at dusk. On full-moon nights, the silver light makes it float away against the star-spangled sky. Monsoon clouds give it a moody blue tint and it appears and disappears like a mirage in the drifting mists of winter.

It can be solid and earthbound, fragile and ethereal, white, amber, grey and gold. The many faces of Taj Mahal display the seductive power of architecture at its best.

TAJ MUSEUM

Timing:
10 am to 5 pm.
Closed Mondays
and Fridays.

FATEHPUR SIKRI

The City That Time Forgot

An emperor builds a magnificent city as an act of gratitude to a penniless saint, makes it the capital of his empire and then, for some inexplicable reason, abandons it.

Fatehpur Sikri is a city that an emperor forgot. After just fourteen years of life, the palaces of Akbar's great City of Victory fell silent. Its echoing corridors still seem to wait for the king to return.

The hill-top city lies 37 kms from Agra in the state of Uttar Pradesh. This deserted city has two distinct complexes. The first comprises the royal enclosure of the palaces, the harem and official buildings and the second is the *dargah* of a Sufi saint, with a mosque and a lofty gateway.

The *dargah* of the Sufi saint Salim Chishti

To wander among the red sandstone courtyards of Fatehpur Sikri is to travel back in time to when the Mughal emperor Akbar rode through its gateway after a triumphant campaign, to be welcomed by his delighted subjects and the royal court.

By 1568, Akbar, the third monarch of the Mughal dynasty had built himself an impressive empire. His kingdom spanned north India and there was no king who could challenge him. There was peace in the land and the royal treasury overflowed with tribute. His only grief was that, at the age of twenty-six and after twelve years of rule, he had no heir. None of his sons had survived infancy.

When Akbar prayed before the Sufi saint, Sheikh Salim Chishti, the *pir* predicted that the king would have three sons. Chishti lived in a secluded hill-top shack in a village called Sikri, a little removed from Agra. In 1569, one of Akbar's Rajput queens, who later came to be known as Maryam Zamani or Mary of the Age, gave birth to a son.

The sprawling palace complex in Fatehpur Sikri, a city Emperor Akbar built and then, inexplicably, abandoned within 14 years

He was named Salim after the saint. And, as predicted, two other sons were born within the next few years. The Emperor gave thanks with extravagant grandeur. In 1571, Akbar began building a mosque and then a palace complex at Sikri. Gradually the royal court shifted from Agra to the new city. The nobility built their mansions further down the hill and shops lined the road to Agra. To commemorate his conquest of Gujarat, Akbar named his new capital Fatehpur Sikri or the City of Victory.

Ever since Emperor Akbar had his wish for an heir fulfilled by the Sufi mystic, Salim Chishti, devotees have thronged to tie a thread at the saint's *dargah* and pray for their own hearts' desires

The mystery is that after fourteen years of occupation, Akbar moved away from Sikri in 1585 and never returned. He first moved court to Lahore and then chose to return to Agra. Fatehpur Sikri was never again the capital of the Mughal empire.

Scholars have speculated about this sudden departure. One theory is that the water supply gave out, but it is hard to believe that Akbar's planners and engineers would have created a city without ensuring something so essential.

The simplest explanation is probably that it was never a conscious decision. Akbar moved north to Lahore to handle a threat to his empire and so on to other capital cities. It was, as historian G.H.R. Tillotson calls it, 'a typical exercise in Mughal prodigality'.

Akbar was the first Mughal king with the means and the opportunity to build extensively.

The facade of Jami Masjid has an arcade of pointed arches, dwarfed by a towering *iwan* or central gate

His predecessors had ruled in uncertain times with Humayun even losing his kingdom for a while. It was Akbar who laid the foundations of an empire and he planned this city as a symbol of his power.

The structures here include palaces and courtyards, as well as official buildings like audience halls, the treasury, the harem, soldier's barracks and kitchens. The attached complex comprises the main mosque, the shrine of Sheikh Salim Chishti and a lofty gateway.

With Akbar begins a distinct style of architecture that blends Islamic and Hindu elements to create something unique. The Islamic architecture of Afghanistan and Persia was marked by precise plans and subdued ornamentation in the form of geometric motifs.The Hindu and Buddhist styles were more florid. The Akbari style which fused the two was born of the king's personal preferences and from his use of Hindu craftsmen, primarily from Gujarat.

The building material of Akbar's time was the robust red sandstone. The next great Mughal builder, Akbar's grandson Shahjahan, showed an increasing preference for the opulent extravagance of marble, culminating in the sublime Taj Mahal.

Fatehpur Sikri reflects the many-faceted character of the man who inspired it. The ruthless empire-builder who enjoyed all the trappings of power and also the liberal, enlightened man who took a passionate interest in every aspect of life, be it religion, literature or the painting of miniatures.

Palace Complex

The royal enclosure houses the main palaces of Fatehpur Sikri and was once the seat of the Mughal empire. Here, among the red sandstone pavilions, gardens and courtyards, were Akbar's personal palaces, the harem and some state buildings.

This palace complex remains a riddle to historians. Contemporary accounts seldom identify the structures so that the purpose of each palace is today a matter of pure conjecture. Moreover, some palaces have gained names and legends spun in the fertile minds of the local tourist guides.

Diwan-i-Am or the Hall of Public Audience is the first building beyond the entrance. It is a pillared pavilion in red sandstone facing a large courtyard surrounded by a colonnaded corridor. It was one of the earliest structures to be finished and, according to contemporary accounts like the *Akbarnama,* it served a variety of purposes.

1. Bamusa Mahal
2. Tomb of Sheikh Salim Chishti
3. Jami Masjid
4. Buland Darwaza
5. Hawa Mahal
6. Jodha Bai's Palace
7. Birbal's House
8. Panch Mahal
9. Ankh Michauli
10. Diwani-i-Khas
11. Pachisi Board
12. Turkish Sultana's House
13. Khwabgah
14. Diwan-i-Am
15. Mint

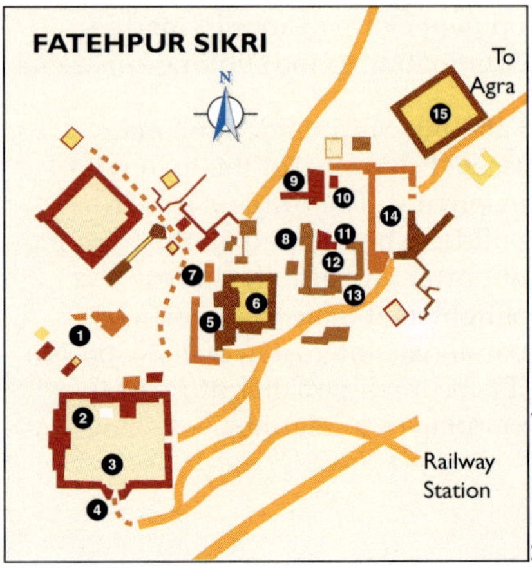

Map not to scale

It was where the Emperor held his daily audiences, where major court activities took place, and where major festivals and events were celebrated, including Prince Salim's wedding to a Hindu princess in 1584. It has beautifully carved *jali* or trellis screens with Islamic geometric designs and Hindu touches in the floral motifs, the *chhajjas* and corbelled capitals.

A small entrance behind the Diwan-i-Am leads into the *mardana* or gentlemans' court. Here are the personal palaces of the king and the official buildings ranged around two connected courtyards. **Diwan-i-Khas** or the Hall of Private Audience stands at the northern end of the first courtyard.

The free-standing Diwan-i-Khas probably had a ceremonial or ritualistic role, rather than being the audience hall tradition says it was

By all accounts, Diwan-i-Khas is the most enigmatic structure of the whole complex. From the exterior it looks like a simple double-storeyed building but it actually has only one floor.

The interior has intrigued historians and archaeologists for centuries. A massive, intricately carved column rises from the centre of the ground floor. The top of the column broadens into a wide circular seat with four catwalks connecting it to the circular galleries that run halfway up the wall.

Tradition says this was Akbar's Diwan-i-Khas where he met ambassadors and governors and heard reports from officials. However the design of the hall does not gel with this. As a matter of fact, many other buildings in the complex have also been identified as the Diwan-i-Khas.

Historians have been greatly intrigued by the unusual shape of the central column. Some see it as the Tree of Life, others as a Hindu *mandala*. Some feel this was, in fact, the Jewel House mentioned in many contemporary chronicles, while others say this was the famous Ibadat Khana, where Akbar met religious leaders for discussions. The chief product of Akbar's religious study was a new religion, the Din-i-Ilahi, which drew together ideas from disparate sources.

The pillar in the Diwan-i-Khas that has been interpreted variously as symbolising the Tree of Life or even the Hindu concept of the *mandala*

A view through the marble *jali* screen surrounding the *dargah*

A detail of the *jali* screens in the Panch Mahal. The lattice-work screens allowed the women of the harem to look out without being themselves seen by outsiders

The hall to the west of the Diwan-i-Khas is rather imaginatively called **Ankh Michauli** and the local guides weave romantic tales of how the king played *ankh michauli* or blind man's buff here with the women of the harem. It is hard to imagine a busy king like Akbar at play and, moreover, this palace is in the *mardana* section where the women would not venture.

A stronger possibility is that it was the treasury. The elaborately ornamented kiosk outside called the Astrologer's Seat was probably the post of Akbar's principal treasurer, Phul Malik. This is even more plausible if you identify the next building, the Diwan-i-Khas as the Jewel House.

Facing the Pachisi Court where Akbar is said to have played the board game of *pachisi* with maids as human counters, is the most eye-catching structure in Fatehpur Sikri – the delicately-columned hall rising five storeys, called the **Panch Mahal**. Every level diminishes in size until there is just one four-columned kiosk at the top. The carvings on the pillars have a wide variety of motifs and, originally, the space between the pillars was covered by *jali* screens. It was probably a building used for social occasions and, despite its height, the structure has a light and airy appearance.

The next courtyard has a delightful ornamental pool called the **Anup Talao** that faces the double-storeyed private palace of the emperor called the **Khwabgah** or Palace of Dreams. Legend has it that the royal court singer Tansen used to perform from the seat in the centre of the pool.

Right:
Panch Mahal

To the north of the Anup Talao is the **Turkish Sultana's House**, believed to be the residence of a Turkish queen. However, it is unlikely that a queen's palace would be situated outside the harem complex. This pavilion was probably one of the king's personal palaces. It is a square room surrounded by a verandah with a sloping roof. The walls and columns are covered in floral and geometric patterns.

The Turkish Sultana's House: It could hardly be the palace of a queen for it is situated outside the *zenana*

The main palace of the *zenana* or harem is called **Jodha Bai's Palace** after Akbar's Rajput queen. However, harem life was communal and it is unlikely that a single queen would have used such a huge palace. It was probably the residence of several of Akbar's principal wives.

The plain, stark exterior hides the private world of an open courtyard, surrounded by apartments for the women. The roof is covered with startling sky blue tiles, seldom seen in Mughal buildings.

Jodha Bai's Palace: The main palace of the *zenana*

As the plan of the interior and the decorations resemble many Rajput palaces, especially the Gwalior Fort, it is possible that Akbar built the palace for the Rajput princesses in his harem.

There is a screened pavilion by the northern wall called the **Hawa Mahal**, where the women could sit in seclusion enjoying the view and the cool breezes.

To the west of Jodha Bai's Palace is an elaborately decorated palace that the local guides claim was the residence of Akbar's adviser and confidante Raja Birbal. This is unlikely as no one outside the royal family would have been allowed to live within the palace enclosure.

Going by the richness of design, the two apartments were probably occupied by Akbar's senior queens, Ruqayya Begum and Salima Sultan Begum. What distinguishes this structure is the intricate maze of carvings and the *jharokhas,* brackets and pilasters typical of Hindu architecture.

Birbal's House:
The pavilion is mistakenly named for Raja Birbal. Although a valued advisor of Akbar, he would never have been allowed a residence in the royal enclosure. The building was probably just another palace for Akbar's rather large harem.

Dargah Complex

The spiritual centre of Fatehpur Sikri is the shrine of Sheikh Salim Chishti. In fact, the great congregational mosque, the Jami Masjid, was completed in 1571, even before work on the palaces had begun. The *dargah* complex is usually entered by the eastern gateway, the Badshahi Darwaza or the royal gateway, so called because the Emperor used it when coming from the palace to join the congregational prayers. Through the gateway one enters the great expanse of the courtyard of the mosque. To the left is the mammoth Buland Darwaza, while a little ahead to the right is the ethereal marble tomb of Sheikh Salim Chishti.

Inside the Jami Masjid: For nearly a decade after it was built, Emperor Akbar took an active interest in the functioning of the Jami Masjid, even to the extent of sweeping its floors and leading the prayers himself

Jami Masjid

The mosque was conceived as the largest in the kingdom. The vast prayer area in red sandstone is surrounded by cells for the *mullahs* or priests. The entrance from the palaces is from the east and the prayer hall stands to the west. The hall has three domes and the entrance is an arched *iwan*. The roof is fringed by a row of domed *chhatris*. In each of the seven bays, there are three *mihrabs* or recesses marking the direction of the Ka'aba in the holy city of Mecca to which every Muslim must turn in prayer.

The Jami Masjid was intended by Emperor Akbar to capture the spiritual essence of the home of Sheikh Salim Chishti

Dargah of Sheikh Salim Chishti

At the heart of Akbar's city is the marble shrine of Sheikh Salim Chishti. It is one of the most significant Sufi shrines of the region and one of the finest and most famous examples of marble work anywhere in the world. The entrance has four slim pillars with unusual serpentine struts that curve upwards to the roof.

The cenotaph of Salim Chishti's tomb is covered by a canopy decorated with mother-of-pearl.

The jewel-like tomb has delicately carved screens enclosing the verandah that create a serene ambience of dappled light and shade. It is on these *jalis* that the faithful tie their threads when they throng the *dargah,* seeking the fulfilment of their wishes.

The Arabic writing in relief around the outer wall of the tomb chamber are verses from the *Koran* of special significance to Sufis. The floor of the chamber is paved with white marble, inlaid with stones of different colours. The cenotaph has a canopy of glistening mother-of-pearl.

The *jalis* and serpentine struts that support the sloping *chhajjas* of the *dargah* verandah

A *qawwal* singer outside the *dargah*

Often you will see bands of men with musical instruments sitting in the courtyard next to the *dargah.* They are the *qawwal* singers who make the evenings magical with their folk-styled songs of devotion or *qawwaalis.*

Buland Darwaza

The gigantic gateway Akbar named Buland Darwaza or the Lofty Gate looms over the courtyard. It is the greatest architectural monument of Akbar's entire reign. Fatehpur Sikri, whether approached from Agra or Bharatpur is dominated by this stupendous structure.

The Emperor built it after conquering Gujarat in 1573. The Darwaza rises to a height of 40 metres and is topped by pillars and *chhatris*. It is the most Islamic structure in Fatehpur Sikri and echoes early Mughal design with simple ornamentation, the carved verses from the *Koran* and soaring arches. On the outside a long flight of steps sweeps down the hill, giving the gateway additional height.

EXCURSIONS

Bharatpur: The World Heritage Site, Keoladeo Ghana National Park provides marvellous exposure to more than 350 species of birds. Bharatpur, 19 kms from Fatehpur Sikri, is the only wintering ground in India of the endangered Siberian Crane. The finest way to explore the sanctuary is on bicycles or cycle rickshaws both of which can be hired at the entrance.

Buland Darwaza: Emperor Akbar added the lofty gate to the mosque in 1576 to celebrate his conquest of Gujarat

Distinctive Hindu embellishment on Buland Darwaza

GETTING THERE

By Air:
Agra, 37 kms away, is the nearest airport. Delhi's international airport is 204 kms away.

By Rail:
Agra is the nearest railhead.

By Road
Agra 37 kms away and Delhi 204 kms away are connected by excellent roads

Entry fee: Rs 5
Free on Fridays.

Best time to visit:
November to February

SANCHI

The Stupa on a Lonely Hill

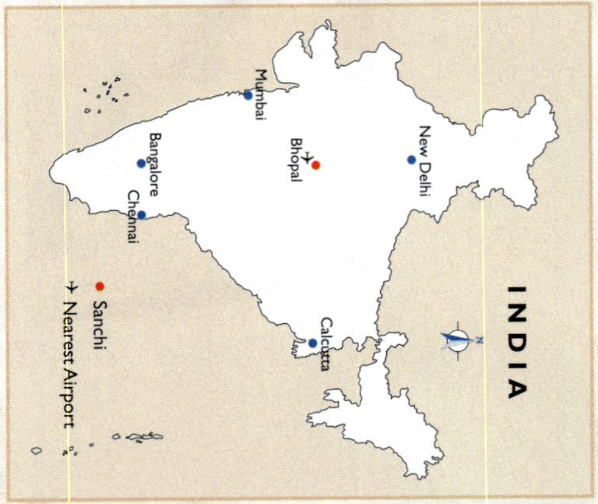

The giant, red dome on top of the hill dominates the peaceful countryside with benign majesty. More than any other monument, the Great Stupa at Sanchi symbolises the rise and spread of Buddhism in India.

Sanchi is located in the district of Raisen in Madhya Pradesh, 46 kms from the state capital of Bhopal. The ruins of *stupas*, temples and monasteries that lie strewn across the hill recall the time when Buddhism had spread across the land and the monasteries at Sanchi teemed with monks and lay worshippers.

The Great Stupa

Sanchi is the largest site of Buddhist remains in India. However, unlike most other Buddhist pilgrimages, it is not directly connected to the life of the Buddha. Its 1,300 years of history chronicle the rise and decline of Buddhism in India.

Originally, *stupas* were built over the relics of the Buddha or at sites important to his life. Later Emperor Ashoka (273 - 236 BC) is said to have built 84,000 *stupas* and renovated many more, of which the Sanchi *stupas* are the best known. These were built in brick and covered in plaster.

Northern Gateway: details of architecture

1. Buddhist Guest House
2. PWD Bungalow
3. Museum & Ticket Office
4. Monastery structure
5. MPTDC Travellers Lodge
6. Stupa-2
7. Great Monastery
8. Great Stupa
9. Stupa-3
10. Temple-31
11. Monastery 46-47
12. Monastery & Temple-45
13. Temple-44
14. Mauryan Temple-40
15. Monastery-38
16. Monastery-3
17. Monastery-36
18. *Chaitya* Hall
19. Gupta Temple
20. Ashoka Pillar
21. Temple-44

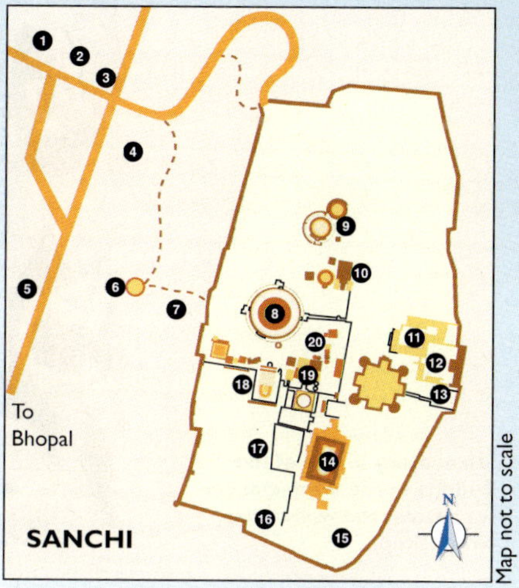

In Sanchi Ashoka built a *stupa* and erected a pillar. The site on the Vidishagiri Hill was ideal for a religious sanctuary. Its picturesque setting gave it both prominence and an atmosphere of seclusion and peace. It was near the prosperous city of Vidisha, whose pious citizens were eager to endow the building work. Vidisha was a great commercial centre on the North-South trading route or the *dakshinapatha*. As a majority of Buddhists came from the merchant classes, Sanchi was patronised by the citizens of Vidisha as well as visitors to the city, and it was being constantly enlarged due to the munificence of these mercantile people.

As a prince, Ashoka had been the governor of Ujjaini and had married a merchant's daughter of nearby Vidisha. Later Ashoka's son Mahendra stopped at Vidisha on his way to Sri Lanka. Here his mother took him to visit a monastery she had endowed at Sanchi.

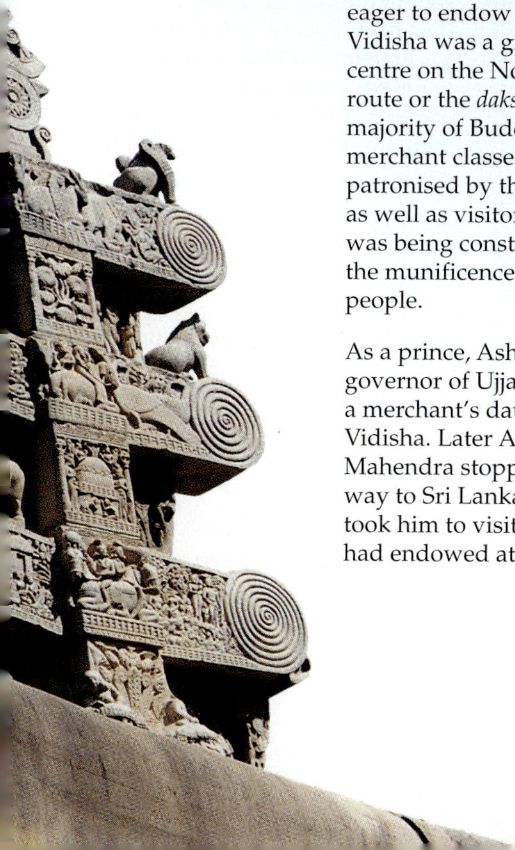

5th century image of the Buddha in the *dhyanamudra* set against the wall of the Great Stupa

GETTING THERE

By Air:
Bhopal (46 kms) is the closest airport. It is linked directly to Mumbai, Delhi and Chennai.

By Rail:
Sanchi has a railway station but it is more convenient to take a train to Bhopal which is connected to all the major cities.

By Road:
Sanchi is a day trip from Bhopal, and is well serviced by buses and taxis.

Entry fee:
Rs 5 per person
Rs 10 to take the car up the hill

Best time to visit:
October to March

After the Mauryas, Sanchi continued to flourish through the Sunga period when Ashoka's brick *stupa* received a casing in stone and a balustrade. Four gateways or *toranas* were added during the reign of the Satavahanas in the first century BC. Four images of the Buddha were added during the reign of the Guptas in the 5th century AD, and one of the oldest surviving Hindu temples of the Gupta period stands here. Some monasteries and temples were built later when the Pratiharas and Paramaras ruled the region.

Monastic activity at Sanchi declined with the gradual disappearance of Buddhism from India. The ruins at Sanchi lay forgotten for over a thousand years until an Englishman, General Taylor, discovered them in 1818. In the initial surge to discover the relics, the monuments were badly damaged and a local landowner broke the Ashoka Pillar in trying to use it as a sugarcane press!

Systematic preservation began only in 1881 and later a small museum was established at the site. Today, the monuments at Sanchi showcase the finest works of Buddhist art and architecture.

The Great Stupa

The Great Stupa (Stupa 1) is one of the oldest *stupas* in India. It can be reached by a half-kilometre drive from the township. There is also a meandering stone stairway for those wishing to walk up to the hilltop.

The *stupa* is a hemispherical dome 36 metres in diameter and 16.46 metres high. The hemispherical dome or the *anda* is the main body. It symbolises the cosmic mountain. A pedestal or *harmika* to hold the triple umbrella or *chhatraveli* tops it. The three circular discs of the *chattraveli* are an auspicious symbol, standing for the *Triratna* or the Three Jewels of Buddhism (the *Buddha*, the *Dharma* and the *Sangha*).

MUSEUM

The Archaeological Survey of India has a museum at the site

Timing:
9 am to 5 pm

Entry fee: Rs 5

Only a broken stump of the Ashoka pillar remains at Sanchi. The pieces lie close to the southern gate of the Great Stupa. The capital with four lions (right) **can be seen at the museum, and it is similar to the famous capital found at Sarnath. The patch of inscription that can still be read on the lower section has Ashoka threatening to excommunicate any monk or nun trying to create schism within the *Sangha*.**

Left:
The themes of the panels on the gateways are scenes from the Jataka tales which relate important episodes from Buddhist history. They also provide an excellent portrait of the life of the period.

The gateways or *toranas* are justly famed for the beauty of their design and intricate carvings. Four *toranas*, each 8.5 metres high, are set at the cardinal points. Many inscriptions on the pavement, gateways and balustrade show they were gifted by lay worshippers.

Stupa 3: Much smaller than the Great Stupa, it contained the relics of two important disciples of the Buddha, Sariputra and Maudgalyayana

Stupa 2 & 3

The hillside is strewn with many big and small votive *stupas*. Stupa 3 stands on the main terrace, 45 metres northeast of Stupa 1 and one of its *toranas* is still intact. Stupa 2 is on a rocky ledge further down the slope and has only a well carved balustrade. The relics inside Stupa 3 were discovered by archaeologist Alexander Cunningham inside large stone boxes with inscriptions on their lid that read *Sariputasa* and *Mahamogalanasa*. The lids are now kept in Sanchi Museum.

Temple 17 is an excellent example of the temple art of the Guptas. It has a flat-roofed *sanctum* and a portico supported by four carved pillars. It has great symmetry and refined ornamentation.

Temples and Monasteries

Temple and Monastery 45 provides a portrait of monastic life in ancient times. Carvings of the Hindu goddesses Ganga and Yamuna prove that Brahmanical motifs had begun to be incorporated in Buddhist buildings by this time. Remains of monks' cells line the courtyard in front.

The only modern building in the area is Chethiyagiri Vihara that stands at the entrance to the complex. The Vihara has been built by the Mahabodhi Society and enshrines the relics found in a *stupa* in nearby Satdhara.

Among the remains of many temples and monasteries the most interesting is Temple 18 facing the south gateway of the Great Stupa. Built in 7th century AD, all that stands are nine elegantly proportioned pillars with architraves, making it oddly classical Greek in style.

Temple and monastery 45 show the remains of a double-storeyed temple with carved doorways and free standing images of the Buddha

Excursions

On the outskirts of Vidisha, 3 kms from the Betwa river, stands the Heliodorus Pillar. The inscription states that the Garuda pillar was erected in 140 BC by Heliodorus, a Greek ambassador, after he embraced Hinduism. Today it is worshipped by the local people as Khamba Baba.

Vidisha, 12 kms away, was an important city in Mauryan times. Standing at the conjunction of the Betwa and Bes rivers it was also known as Besnagar. Ashoka was once a governor of the region and married a lady from Vidisha.

Udaigiri Caves, 16 kms away, are a series of Hindu and Jain caves carved into the sandstone hillside in 4th century AD. One inscription mentions the visit of the Gupta king, Chandragupta Vikramaditya, and says that the caves were made by his Minister of War and Peace, Virasena. Another has an unusual square *linga* and a *mukhalinga* or a *linga* with a face carved on it. The caves have beautifully chiselled entrances, architraves and pillars in the Gupta style.

Satdhara lies on the way from Bhopal to Sanchi. Recent excavations have revealed a large Buddhist complex by the banks of the Bes river.

The majestic Varaha incarnation of Vishnu as a boar in Cave 5 at Udaigiri

KHAJURAHO

Stones of Passion

The temple town of Khajuraho, once the great Chandela capital, is today a village of about a few thousand people in the interiors of central India, in Chhatarpur district of Madhya Pradesh. Tradition records the existence of eighty five temples, of which only twenty five, strewn amidst lakes and fields, have survived. The temples at Khajuraho, brilliant examples of medieval Indian architecture, were built under later Chandela kings between AD 950 and AD 1050. Each ancient structure in India has a fascinating story to tell. But few match the temples of Khajuraho.

Chandela temples of Khajuraho

The name Khajuraho derives from the *khajur* or date palm trees that once surrounded the huge Khajurvahaka Tal. Legend has it that one sultry summer night, Hemvati, the widowed daughter of a minister of the King of Benaras, was bathing in the lake when the Moon God Chandrama saw her and was entranced by her beauty. The son born out of their union was Chandravarman, who grew up to found the Chandela dynasty. In order to atone for his mother's lapse, he raised temples that celebrated the union of *Purush* and *Prakriti*, man and nature, as the source of all life and creation.

The *shikhara* of Kandariya Mahadev Temple: With this temple, the architectural and sculptural movement of Khajuraho reached its peak

Chandela Rajputs rose to power during the early 10th century AD in the land known as Jajhauti, now Bundelkhand. From being local feudatories of the Pratiharas of Kannauj, they rose to become a major power in northern India. They were great patrons of the arts and equally great builders. From 12th century onward, the other rival powers of central India and Muslim invaders like Mahmud Ghazni whom the Chandelas had kept at bay, began reasserting them selves. Al-Biruni, the chronicler of Mahmud Ghazni, mentions Jajhauti with 'Kajuraha' as its capital.

Temple construction continued sporadically until the 12th century. Far removed from the political centre of the kingdom, its location minimised the danger of external attack, making

Khajuraho the Chandelas' spiritual homeland. In 1335 Ibn Batuta talks about 'Kajarra' with a great pond, flanked by temples containing idols and ascetics with matted locks living in them.

The earliest temples of Khajuraho were built in coarse granite. However, the most famous ones – including the World Heritage monuments known as the Western Group of temples – are mostly built in fine-grained buff, pink and pale yellow sandstone, quarried from neighbouring Panna. The temples belong to different religious sects like Shaiva, Vaishnava and Jain and mark the culmination of the northern Indian or Nagara style of temple architecture.

1. Tribal Art Museum
2. Hotel Khajuraho Ashok
3. Tourist Bungalow
4. Circuit House
5. MP Tourism
6. Tourist Village
7. Chitragupta Temple
8. Jagadambi Temple
9. Kandariya Mahadev Temple
10. Vishvanath Temple
11. Lakshmana Temple
12. Matangeshwara Temple
13. Tourist Office
14. Museum
15. Gol Market
16. Chausath Yogini Temple
17. Bus stand
18. Post Office
19. Hotel Jass Oberoi
20. Hotel Taj Chandela
21. Indian Airlines
22. Hotel Clarks Bundela
23. Hotel Clarks Khajuraho
24. Hotel Holiday Inn
25. Dulhadev Temple
26. Jain Temples
27. Ghanta Temple
28. Javan Temple
29. Brahma Temple
30. Vaman Temple

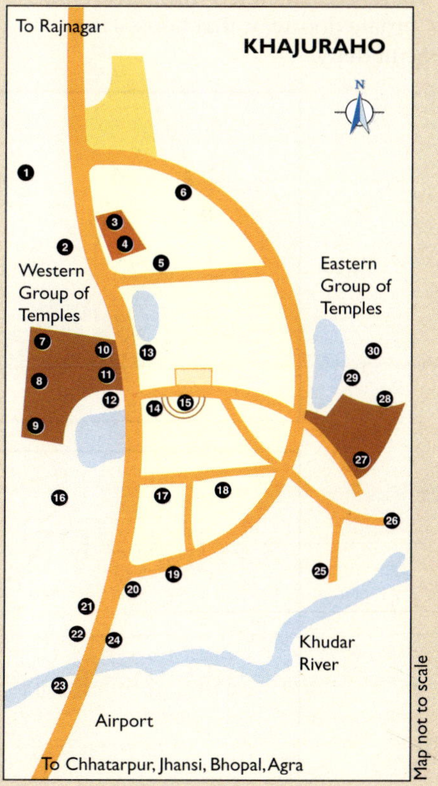

A typical Khajuraho temple sits upon a lofty stone terrace called the *adisthana* or *jagati*, over which rise the *jangha* or walls of the inner compartments. It also has canopied windows with balconies to admit air and light into the interior. The roof comprises turrets of varying heights, culminating in the tall and graceful curvilinear *shikhara* suggesting rising mountain peaks.

Right:
Lakshmana temple:
Like other temples of the Western Group it is erected on a lofty terrace. Windows with overhanging eaves form beautiful openings for the inner compartments.

The Khajuraho temples are almost all aligned east to west, with the entrance facing east. A profusely carved arch leads to the oblong porch or *ardhamandapa*, behind which is the large assembly hall or *mandapa*, open on three sides, followed by the still larger hall *mahamandapa*, a closed hall with a corridor around it. This hall finally leads into the vestibule or the *antarala*. Beyond this is the *garbhagriha* or *sanctum*, entered through another ornate doorway, that houses the cult deity.

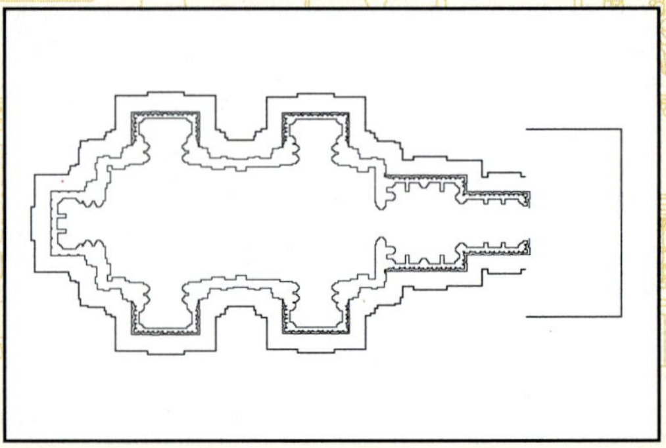

The larger temples have both inner and outer ambulatory passages or *sandharas*. And some have subsidiary shrines on the four corners making the structure a *panchayatna* or five-shrined complex. Both the interiors and the exterior are beautifully carved. A series of friezes runs right round the temple, from the basement to the projections and the recesses of the walls above. The inside walls, doorways, pillars, pilasters, niches, architraves and ceilings all display a wealth of ornamentation which has few parallels.

The sculptors of Khajuraho have shown immense virtuosity in expressing the myriad aspects of Indian life – gods and goddesses, guardians of the quarters, sensuous and graceful *apsaras* (nymphs), *surasundaris* (attendants of higher divinities), *salabhanjikas* (tree nymphs) in infinite moods and postures.

It is the amorous couples of Khajuraho, appearing mostly on the panels of the *sandhara* temples, that have drawn maximum attention. Their gestures and expressions pulsate with life and exhibit great passion, sensitivity, joy and warmth.

Ten centuries after they were constructed, these temples remain a celebration of life

Traditionally, love or *kama*, symbols of life and creation, had religious sanction as one of the aims or pursuits of life, along with *dharma* or piety and *artha* or economic pursuit. The full attainment of all three leads to *moksha* or salvation. Depictions of *mithuna* or loving human couples were seen as auspicious signs of fertility that would ward off evil and bestow great merit on the builder when used in architecture.

The existing temples of Khajuraho can be divided into three groups, Western, Eastern and Southern. The famous Western group, designated a World Heritage site, is enclosed within a beautifully laid-out park. The Lakshmana and Vishvanath temples to the front and the Kandariya Mahadev, Jagdambi and Chitragupta temples at the rear, showcase the best of Khajuraho.

Considered a brilliant episode in the history of Indian temple architecture, the Khajuraho sculptures reveal the sensuous charms of the human body

Western Group

Lakshmana Temple is closest to the entrance of the complex. Various incarnations of Vishnu and his consort Lakshmi and the planets can be seen on the *sanctum* doorway. Popular legends from Krishna's life are engraved on the walls. One of the main niches enshrines a three-headed and four-armed image of Vishnu.

The temple boasts the largest number of *apsara* brackets. Two bands of sculpture sporting a profusion of erotic scenes run around the temple. On the subsidiary shrine at the southwest corner, one can see an architect working with his students and this is conjectured to be the temple's designer.

Vishvanath Temple to the northeast is another finely developed temple built by King Dhanga in early 11th century. The *sanctum* once enshrined two Shiva *lingas*, one of emerald and the other of stone, but only the latter remains. Facing the temple is a pavilion with a colossal Nandi bull, Shiva's favoured vehicle. The sculpted bands on the walls show seven mother goddesses with Ganesha and Virbhadra. To the southwest of the main shrine stands a small Parvati temple.

Lakshmana temple: One of the best preserved temples in the complex, this *panchayatna* temple (with all four subsidiary shrines extant) was built between AD 930 and AD 950 by King Yashovarman and is dedicated to Vishnu

The small Varaha temple is directly opposite the Lakshmana temple. Built in the early part of the 10th century, it is a sandstone structure placed on a lofty plinth. It enshrines a colossal, intricately carved image of Varaha, Vishnu's boar incarnation.

Towards the rear of the Western Group stands the largest and most impressive temple of Khajuraho – **Kandariya Mahadev**. Although its subsidiary shrines have long disappeared, the central shrine is in superb condition. It has the loftiest plinth and the largest number of projections and recesses. The lofty *shikhara* towers to a height of 31 metres. Both the interior and the exterior are exquisitely carved with figures of gods and goddesses, warriors and musicians, hunters and mythical animals, as well as the famed images of sexual union that have intrigued visitors through the ages. Stone figures of sensual celestial maidens and nubile beauties appear here in great profusion, as do erotic figures of men and women. On the same plinth stands a small Shiva temple.

The incredibly beautiful stonework on the temples has made them a legacy worth cherishing

Kandariya Mahadev Temple was built by King Vidyadhari between AD 1025-50

The comparatively small **Jagdambi Devi** temple shares the same plinth as the Kandariya Mahadev but is older. Its square ceiling is richly embellished and the external walls have some of the finest figures of gods and goddesses, *surasundaris* and erotic couples.

North of Jagdambi Devi temple is **Chitragupta**, the only temple in Khajuraho dedicated to Surya, the sun god, that dates to AD 1000-25.

Jagdambi Devi: Originally dedicated to Vishnu it now enshrines a Parvati image

An ornate doorway leads to the *sanctum* which enshrines a standing image of Surya riding a chariot of seven horses. The basement moulding shows a processional frieze of dancing girls, hunting scenes, and elephant fights.

Just outside the Western Group enclosure on the bank of the Shivsagar tank, stands the Matangeshvara Temple, the only temple in Khajuraho still functioning. Dedicated to Shiva, it houses a large Gauripatta holding a massive *linga*, 2.5 metres high

Eastern Group

This group of temples is situated around Khajuraho village. It includes the 9th century **Brahma Temple** standing on the banks of Ninora lake, with a four-faced Shiva *linga* that is commonly mistaken for Brahma, the god with four faces. To the northeast of the Brahma Temple is the beautiful **Vamana Temple** dating to AD 1050-75, dedicated to the dwarf incarnation of Vishnu. It is famous for its graceful figures and exquisite *chaitya* arches. Two hundred metres south is an architectural gem, the **Javari Temple** dedicated to Vishnu. Its ornate gateway, the *makara torana,* and slender *shikhara* are especially noteworthy.

The neighbouring **Ghantai Temple** (named for the chain and bell motifs carved on its tall pillars) is a Jain temple. Only an entrance porch and a *mahamandapa* with a flat ornate ceiling survive. Southeast stand some more Jain temples: Adinath, Parshvanath and the only functional Jain shrine, the **Santinath Temple**, with a colossal image of Tirthankara Adinath. The **Parshvanath** is one of the best temples, not only in the group but in Khajuraho. Built during King Dhanga's reign, it is a solid structure with graceful sculpture dedicated to the first Jaina Tirthankara. It displays superb figures of Hindu gods and goddesses and some of the loveliest celestial beauties.

Southern Group

This group comprises **Duladeo Temple** with its strikingly large *mandapa* and exquisite figures, and **Chaturbhuj Temple** to the southwest of the Jatkira village that houses a huge image of the four-armed Dakshinamurti Shiva.

Just behind Chaturbhuj, the Archaeological Survey of India has begun excavating a new site in March 1999 which has revealed a temple with a plinth of 34 metres, pointing to a temple larger even than the Kandariya Mahadev. Known as **Bijamandala,** this mound lies 4 kms to the southeast of the Western Group. A broken marble *yonipatta* pedestal with a marble Shiva *linga* caps the mound. Several carvings of the Jain Tirthankaras have also been discovered in the temple which seems to have been abandoned before completion.

Art historians have conjectured that the plan of the *sanctum* of the temple at Bijamandala has similarities with that of the Kandariya Mahadev. The mound has also yielded a treasure trove of antiquities including sculptures of Mahishasuramardini, Vamana, Yamuna and figurines of bulls, besides a graceful image of the goddess Saraswati.

Entry fee: Rs 5

Admission free on Fridays

Timing:
Open from sunrise to sunset

Good guides are available for Rs 250 for half a day.

Best time to visit:

Early morning and late evening are the best time to see the temples.

The **Khajuraho Festival of Dance** draws some of the greatest exponents of classical dance from across India each year.

For over 25 years now, the magnificent structures come alive in early March. Silhouetted against the setting sun, the temples form an exquisite backdrop for the performers. As dusk falls, soft-focus light transforms the temple area into an ethereal stage, on which is celebrated the classical dance tradition of India. The festival, sponsored by Eicher, is a unique treat for connoisseurs from across the world.

Son-et-Lumiere

Every evening:
6.30-7.30 in English
7.30-8.30 in Hindi

Entry Fee:
Rs 200 for foreigners
Rs 50 for Indians

Excursions

Short excursions lead through a beautiful landscape steeped in history and culture.

Visit the Old Fort of **Dhubela** 57 kms away, to see sculptures, weapons and royal effects of the Bundela kings. 80 kms away is the **Ajai Garh** fort, built by the Chandela kings.

Kalinjar Fort, 100 kms away, stands on the last spur of the Vindhya hills. It is among the oldest sites dating to the 2nd century AD Along the drive from Satna to Khajuraho is the **Panna National Park**, set along the Ken river.

Northwest of Khajuraho lies **Orchha**, the ancient capital of the Bundela dynasty, with its temples, palaces and gardens laid out along the Betwa river.

Other short trips are Benisagar dam (7 kms), Raneh falls (20 kms) Gangaur sanctuary (25 kms) Rajgarh palace (25 kms), Ranguan lake (25 kms), Pandav falls (34 kms), Panna diamond mines (56 kms)

GETTING THERE

By Air:
The airport is at Khajuraho

By Rail:
Jhansi (172 kms) and Satna (117 kms) are the major railheads

By Road:
Khajuraho is 590 kms from Delhi via Gwalior and Jhansi

MUSEUM

- The site museum at Khajuraho houses some of the most outstanding objects of Chandela art.

Entrance: Rs 5

- The Tribal Folk Art Museum houses a good collection of folk art from Madhya Pradesh.

Timing:
9 am to 4 pm
Closed Mondays

Entry fee:
Rs 50 for foreigners
Rs 10 for Indians

ELEPHANTA

Many Faces of Shiva

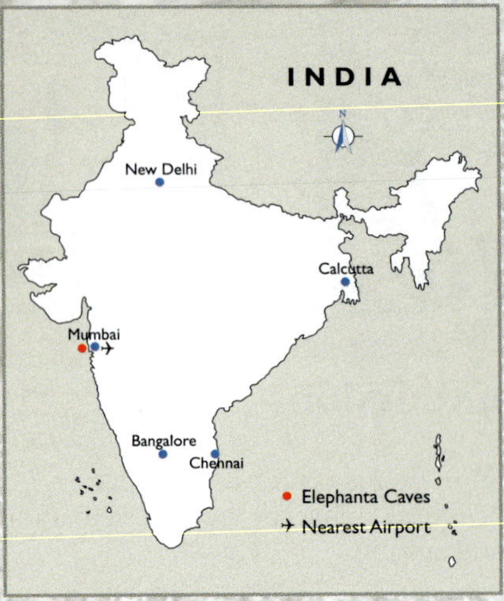

A dark cave on a tiny island, in the middle of Mumbai harbour, houses one of the most imposing examples of early rock-cut architecture. Although not quite as spectacular as the Ajanta or Ellora caves, the Elephanta cave, a 10-km boat ride from the Gateway of India in Mumbai, is well worth a visit.

The cave temple, dedicated to Shiva, was excavated sometime in the 8th century by the Rashtrakuta kings who ruled the area between AD 757-973.

The colossal image of Shiva as Maheshwara

The setting of the Elephanta cave temple was deemed symbolic as the sea represents *samsara,* the turbulent river of life, and the island was, thus, a place of physical and spiritual refuge. Today, it bears little resemblance to a spiritual retreat; the steps up from the jetty are lined with souvenir shops and soft drink stalls and, on the weekend, the island turns into a virtual carnival, with day-trippers from Mumbai coming over in large numbers.

The island, known as Gharapuri or the Fort Town, was christened Elephanta by the Portuguese, who captured it from the Sultan of Gujarat in AD 1535. They named it for its huge sculpted elephant, but treated it with scant concern, turning the pillared *mandapa* into a shooting gallery and letting the famous elephant fall to pieces. The British, who annexed the island in the 1770s, had the broken figure removed to the Victoria Gardens adjoining the Victoria & Albert Museum in Byculla in Mumbai.

1. Shiva as Nataraja
2. Andhakasuravadhamurti Shiva
3. Shiva *Linga*
4. Kalyanasundaramurti
5. Descent of Ganga
6. Maheshwara
7. Shiva as Ardhanarishwara
8. Parvati in attitude of Mana
9. Ravana under Kailasa
10. Shiva as Lakulisa

The cave temple, situated some 75 metres above jetty level, closely follows the pattern of the Dumar Lena cave in Ellora.

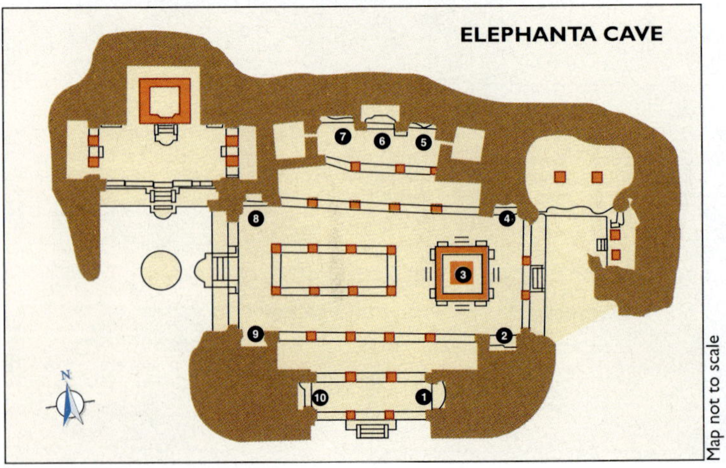

Under this style, an isolated shrine is contained within a group of pillared halls that are arranged on a cruciform plan and have entrances in the wings as well. This allowed light to infiltrate the darkest depth of the cave. At Elephanta, for instance, the main image of Shiva as Maheshwara is so skilfully placed in relation to the three entrances, that it receives just the amount of light necessary to make it look as though the Lord is emerging from eternal darkness.

At Elephanta, elaborate sculptures show Shiva in his myriad moods

This image, placed in a vestibule at the end furthest away from the entrance, is the focus of the entire temple. The cave is devoid of minor decorations, which only heightens the effect of the monumental sculpted panels depicting Shiva in myriad forms.

Step into the foyer of the cave and find a carving of Shiva as Nataraja on your right and as Lakulisa on your left. Created in the Buddhist mould, the sculpture shows Lakulisa, a 7th century priest who did much to reabsorb Buddhists into Hinduism, seated on a lotus, the symbol of enlightenment.

The *garbhagriha* has entrances at the four cardinal points. Giant *dwarapalas* and their *gana* attendants guard these doorways. The shrine itself has a metre-high *linga*.

At the four corners of the main *mandapa* are the famous wall panels showing Shiva in many moods. Across the width of the hall is a representation of, *kalayanasundaram*, the marriage of Shiva with Parvati. A coy Parvati and a confidant Shiva are surrounded by her father Himalaya, the moon-god Chandrama, Brahma and Vishnu.

Right across the *mandapa* is a scene from the domestic life of Shiva and Parvati. The divine couple are shown playing dice. Parvati has obviously lost the game and is sulking prettily while her husband tries to woo her back to the game.

On the wall across from the entrance is the cave's centrepiece, the triple-headed figure of Shiva as Maheshwara or Lord of the Universe.

GETTING THERE

Maharashtra Tourism launches, with good guides on board, leave the Gateway of India every 30 mins from 9 am. Last return from Elephanta at 5.30 pm. The journey takes 1½ hours and costs Rs 50. Service is suspended from June to September. Faster catamarans are also available.

One of the eight panels depicting Lord Shiva with his consort, Parvati

Enormous *dwarapalas* guard the four entrances to the shrine

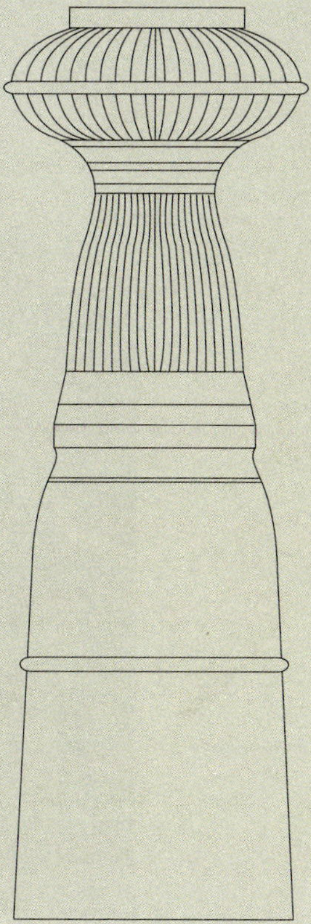

Standing high at 5.45 metres, the *Trimurti* statue depicts the three aspects of Shiva as creator, preserver and destroyer. The head on the left is generally believed to be that of Shiva's life-giving *shakti*, Uma, while the one on the right shows him as Rudra-Bhairava, a fearful figure with snakes in his hair. The central face is the *swarupa* or true self of Shiva – calm, serene and with his right hand (now broken) raised in benediction.

The enclosures contain a carving of Shiva as Ardhanarishwara – in which he combines the female and the male aspects in his own self – and a panel depicting the descent of the heavenly river Ganga to earth. Here, Ganga is shown in the company of her two tributaries, the Yamuna and the Saraswati.

FESTIVAL

Maharashtra Tourism organises a festival of classical music and dance in the third week of February

AJANTA CAVES

Chaityas and Viharas

Way back in 1819, a party of British army officers on a tiger hunt in the forests of the western Deccan, suddenly spotted their prey, on the far side of a loop in the Waghora river. High up on the horseshoe-shaped cliff, the hunting party saw the tiger, silhouetted against the carved facade of a cave.

On investigating, the officers discovered a series of carved caves, each more dramatic than the other. Hewn painstakingly as monsoon retreats or *varshavasas* for Buddhist monks, the cave complex was continuously lived in from 200 BC to about AD 650. There are thirty caves, including some unfinished ones. Of the Ajanta caves, five are *chaityas* or prayer halls and the rest are *viharas* or monasteries.

The facade of Cave 10, the earliest excavation at Ajanta

The paintings in the Ajanta caves capture the carnival of life

The Ajanta caves resolve themselves into two phases, separated from each other by a good four hundred years. These architectural phases coincide with the two schools of Buddhist thought, the older Hinayana school where the Buddha was represented only in symbols like the *stupa*, a set of footprints or a throne; and the later Mahayana sect which did not shy away from giving the Lord a human form.

Among the more prominent Hinayana caves are those numbered 9, 10 (both *chaityas*), 8,12, 13 and 15 (all *viharas*). The sculpted figures in these caves are dressed and coiffed in a manner reminiscent of the *stupas* at Sanchi and Barhut, indicating that they date back to the first or second century BC.

The Mahayana monasteries include 1, 2, 16 and 17, while the *chaityas* are in caves 19 and 26. The caves, incidentally, are not numbered chronologically but in terms of access from the entrance. A terraced path of modern construction connects the caves, but in ancient times, each cave was accessed from the riverfront by individual staircases.

The panoramic sweep of the Ajanta caves

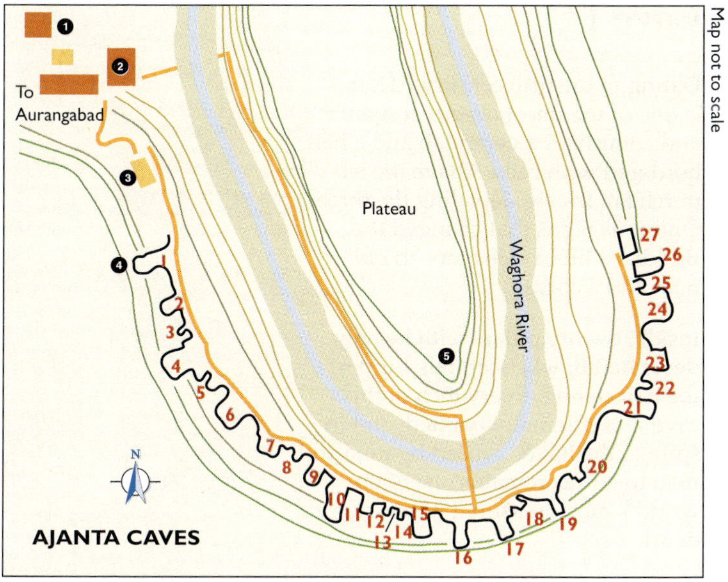

The sculptures and paintings in the caves detail the Buddha's life as well as the lives of the Buddha in his previous births, as related in the allegorical Jataka tales. You will also find in the caves a sort of illuminated history of the times – court scenes, street scenes, cameos of domestic life and even animal and bird studies come alive on these unlit walls.

1. MPTDC Resort & Restaurant
2. Souvenir Shops
3. Ticket Counter
4. Caves
5. View Point

Cave 1

Dating to the fifth century AD, this is one of the finest *viharas* at Ajanta and comprises a verandah and a hall bordered with cells. Above the left porch are friezes depicting the three Ominous Signs that changed the Buddha's life: a sick man, an old man and a corpse.

Inside, twenty pillars with heavily decorated bracket-capitals support the hall ceiling. Every inch of this cave was originally painted, and in spite of the havoc caused by time and man to it, this remains one of the world's most treasured possessions of art.

The *sanctum* to the rear has a colossal image of the Buddha in the *dharmachakra pravartana mudra* or the preaching pose. What is amazing is the sculptor's skill conveys different moods of the Buddha – solemn and contemplative when seen from your left, joyful from the right and tranquil when viewed from the front.

Left:
The Padmapani:
This painted figure of a compassionate Boddhisattava from Cave 1 remains an enduring image of the Ajanta caves

This cave contains some of the best known paintings of Ajanta, with the masterpieces flanking the entrance to the shrine chamber. On the left is Padmapani, the compassionate Boddhisattva with a lotus in his hand and on the right, with his brilliantly bejewelled headgear, is the Bodhisattava Vajrapani.

The side-walls of the antechamber are painted with murals showing two important episodes from the Buddha's life: the left wall narrates the story of Gautama being tempted by Mara just before he became the Buddha. The right wall depicts the miracle of Sravasti, where in order to confound heretics and disbelievers, the Buddha multiplied himself into thousand images.

The walls of the main hall are painted with representations of a large number of Jatakas, the stories of the previous births of Gautama Buddha.

Vajrapani:
The delicacy of hand that created the murals is evident in this painting of a Boddhisattava from Cave I

The ancient artists of Ajanta covered the rough rock walls with a layer of mud and cow dung, mixed with straw or animal hair as a binding medium. This layer was an inch or an inch-and-a-half thick and, when dry, was smoothened over with a layer of sieved gypsum or lime plaster. It was upon this that the painters created their worlds of colour.

The paintings in the Ajanta caves are often mistakenly referred to as frescoes. A fresco refers to the application of colours to moist lime plaster. At Ajanta, the paintings were done on dry wall.

Another amazing fact about the paintings is that they were done in extremely poor light in the caves. Only very diffused rays of sunlight penetrate the caves, making it difficult to even figure out the murals, let alone paint them.

Various theories have been advanced about how they were completed, ranging from the use of oil lamps, to the use of mirrors to reflect and magnify the little natural light there was. According to an ingenious theory, the depression in the floor of the main chambers, a feature of all caves, was filled with water, which caught the few rays that did reach into the darkness.

However, it seems unlikely that any of these methods could have generated enough light for the minute and detailed work that adorns the Ajanta walls.

Cave 2

Cave 2 is remarkable for its painted ceiling that gives the effect of a cloth canopy, right down to the slight sag in the middle. The *mandala* or circular diagram of the cosmos is supported by demons.

The walls of the various chambers in the cave are adorned with countless Buddhas in various poses and a painted record on the rear wall of the ante-chamber tells of the donation that funded these 'thousand painted Buddhas'.

Cave 9

One of the earliest caves, dating around first century BC, this *chaitya* has a vaulted ceiling that was originally supported by wooden beams. The holes where these beams fitted can still be seen. The roof arches from a huge ribbed *chaitya* window. Some of the paintings recall the style of Sanchi but there are also later murals depicting the Buddha in person.

Cave 10

The earliest excavation of Ajanta, this cave is dated to second century BC by an inscription, now destroyed, recording a royal donation. It has a double-storeyed *stupa* similar to that of Cave 9.

Cave 16

One of the most beautiful *viharas* of Ajanta, it has a detailed inscription on the left outer wall, recording its antecedents. Varahadeva, a minister

GETTING THERE

By Air:
Chikalthana airport at Aurangabad (106 kms) is the nearest airfield and is directly linked to Mumbai, Delhi, Jaipur and Udaipur

By Rail:
Aurangabad, the closest railhead, is directly connected to Mumbai, Delhi, Agra and Bhopal. Alternatively, you can take a bus or taxi to Jalgaon (59 kms), a mainline junction from where you get faster express trains to Mumbai and Delhi.

By Road:
Aurangabad is connected to all major cities and towns by good roads. The Maharashtra State Road Transport Corporation runs ordinary and luxury buses from here to Mumbai (392 kms).

of the Vakataka king, Harisena (c AD 475-500), funded it for the specific use of the 'best of ascetics'. The record also lists its various attractions including ornamented doors, windows, pillars, statues of celestial nymphs, stairs and a shrine and *mandapa*. Most of the paintings have now faded.

Cave 17

Apart from an elaborately-carved doorway, what makes this cave especially remarkable is the number of murals that have survived. The masterpieces include the panel above the doorway depicting the seven Manushi Buddhas (Buddhas in human form) together with the Maitreya or Future Buddha, seated under their respective Bodhi trees.

Directly below the row of Buddhas, is a line of eight loving or *mithuna* couples in varied styles of dress and coiffures.

The painted panels on the back wall of the verandah are relatively well preserved. A particularly beautiful one is of the king of gods flying amidst clouds with his entourage of celestial nymphs or *apsaras* and musicians. The figures of the *apsaras* on the right of the doorway express the consummate skill of the painters, which is apparent even in their damaged state. Most beautiful of them all is the figure of the dark-skinned *apsara* with her turban-like headgear.

The walls of the hall inside are embellished with various Jatakas. A noteworthy mural is the one covering the entire left wall between the two pilasters, depicting the Vessantara Jataka that tells of Vessantara's generosity.

Even in a damaged state, this *apsara* from the verandah of Cave 17 is alluring in her beauty

Cave 19

This *chaitya* is noted for its well proportioned elegance. Although one of the later fifth century excavations, it sticks to the traditional plan, with two rows of pillars leading up to and encircling the *stupa* at the rear. The only departure from the older plan is in the image of the Buddha on the *stupa*.

Timing:
9 am to 5 pm
Except Mondays and national holidays

Best time to visit:
October to March, although the monsoon months of July-August are also highly recommended for the heightened scenic beauty of the area.

Cave 26

This *chaitya* is larger than Cave 19 but is similar to it in decoration and arrangement. It is rich in embellishments, with 26 pillars running to curve around a rather stylised *stupa*. However, the *stupa* itself does not draw attention as does the figure of the Buddha seated in the *pralambha-pada* position in front of it under a pavillion. The wall sculptures are quite detailed with the most impressive being the colossal 9-metre figure of the Parinirvana Buddha reclining on his right side between two *saal* trees. Below are figures of his followers mourning his passing away and above are the celestial beings.

Parinirvana Buddha in Cave 26

ELLORA CAVES

Halls of Worship

Nestled in the crook of the Charnadari Hill in the Deccan is a series of ancient temples and monasteries hewn out of the moutainside. Situated on the ancient north-south trade route or the *dakshinapatha*, the tiny mountain village of Verul – mutated today to Ellora – was a well-known stopover for traders, priests and pilgrims who plied the route to the western ports.

Beginning sometime in the 7th century, when the Chalukyas (AD 553 - 753) ruled the Deccan, these wayfarers decided to make their presence permanent. And excavation started on a number of Buddhist *chaityas* and *viharas*. The place found favour with missionaries of other faiths as well, and over the next five centuries, Hindus and Jains also built their temples in the rocks there.

Kailasa Temple or Cave 16

Unlike the caves at Ajanta, the Ellora caves were never 'lost'. Largely because it lay on a more frequented route, Ellora remained in the public eye. In fact, Kailasa Temple remained a practising shrine until the 19th century. Several travellers to India including the 10th century Arab geographer Al Masudi and Niccolao Manucci in early 17th century mention the caves in their accounts.

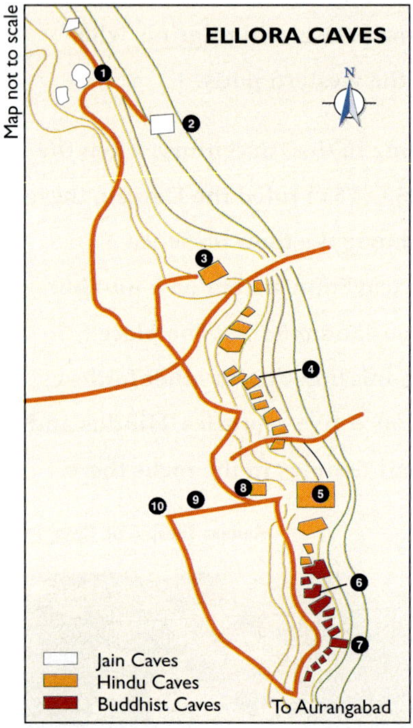

1. Indrasabha
2. Chhota Kailasa
3. Dumar Lena
4. Ramesvara
5. Kailasa Temple
6. Viswakarma
7. Maharwada
8. MTDC Restaurant
9. Kailash Hotel
10. Art Gallery & Restaurant

There are 34 caves, of which 12 are Buddhist, 17 Hindu and 5 Jain. The caves all face west, so are best seen in the afternoon. The Buddhist caves are to your far right as you face the curve of the Charnadari Hill, then come the Hindu ones, and finally, the Jain cave temples to the far left.

Although not too far removed from the Ajanta caves in terms of both space and time, the *chaityas* and *viharas* of Ellora are architecturally and sculpturally different. Compared to the Ajanta paintings and sculptures, the Ellora representations are more earthly, drawing elements from the Vajrayana school of Buddhism which was permeated with primitive ideas of magic and mysticism. So, the *dwarapalas* that flank each doorway, the gigantic Boddhisattavas and their consorts have a robust earthiness about them.

In fact, it is architectural skill rather than sculptural aesthetics that Ellora is noted for. Buddhist Cave 12 or **Tin Tala**, for instance, has a rather plain edifice with unadorned pillars and the sculptured panels are only on the inner walls.

Tin Tala (Three Storeys) or Cave 12 contains interesting iconographic sculptures

But its historical value lies in the fact that human hands fashioned a three-storeyed building from solid rock with such painstaking skill that even the floors and the ceilings are smooth and levelled. Tin Tala cave is a commodious monastery-cum-chapel, with cells enough to house 40 monks. It dates to the Rashtrakuta period in the middle of the 8th century and, in fact, the third floor, which contains the most sculpted decoration, was being excavated even as the Hindus were carving the magnificent Kailasa Temple further along the rock face. The cruciform layout of the third storey in Cave 12 may also be the inspiration behind the Dumar Lena (Cave 29) and the Shiva cave at Elephanta.

Timing:
9 am to 5 pm
Except Mondays and national holidays

Best time to visit:
October to March, although the monsoon months of July-August are also highly recommended for the heightened scenic beauty of the area.

KAILASA TEMPLE

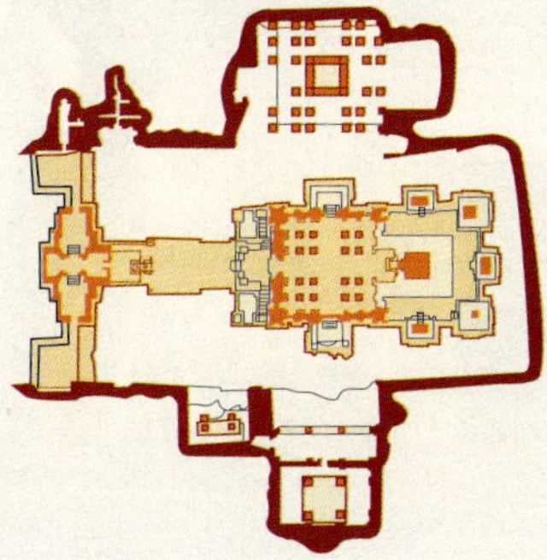

The other Buddhist caves as well as the first few Hindu caves are fairly unremarkable and do not prepare you for the magnificence of **Kailasa Temple** or Cave 16. Believed to have been started by the Rashtrakuta king, Krishna I (AD 756-773), Kailasa Temple is the largest monolithic structure in the world.

Its excavation must rank as an architectural wonder. Two great trenches some 90 metres long were dug into the hillside. They were connected at the deepest point by another trench 53 metres across. The temple was meant to appear as though rising from a vast courtyard at ground level.

Right:
The monumental *dhwajasthamba* in Kailasa Temple

Below:
The entrance to the Nandi *mandapa* of Kailasa Temple. The temple is unique in that its creators sought to sculpt a huge structural monument out of solid rock.

The great block of residual rock, rising 30 metres, was then carved into the three-storeyed *vimana*, the main *mandapa*, two giant *dhwajasthambas* or pillars, and four sub-shrines. Beginning at the top, the mass of rock was hewn into shape, and as each layer was shaped, the carvers began ornamenting the structure. Each layer was thus hewn and decorated completely before moving downward, thus eliminating the need for any scaffolding.

Narrative friezes adorn the walls of Kailasa Temple

Below:
Kailasa Temple has an unusually high plinth covered with intricate sculptures

The temple is dedicated to Shiva and named for his mountain home in the Himalayas, the snow-peak Kailasa. The main shrine and the Nandi *mandapa* are built on a plinth, over 7.8 metres high, with its entire vertical surface carved with mythical animals and gargoyles.

The main temple is flanked on either side by two free-standing pillars, soaring some 15.9 metres high. These gracefully proportioned pillars are believed to have once borne the *trishul* or trident of Shiva.

Two storeys of corridors have been carved into the mountain, ringing the temple on three sides. These corridors are studded with small alcoves, all containing a wealth of sculpted figures telling the tales of the great Hindu epics, the *Mahabharata* and the *Ramayana*. Among the narrative friezes is the descent of river Ganga, and one of Ravana shaking Mount Kailasa. The architectural style and intricate sculpture is similar to Virupaksha Temple at Pattadakal that had been completed a decade before.

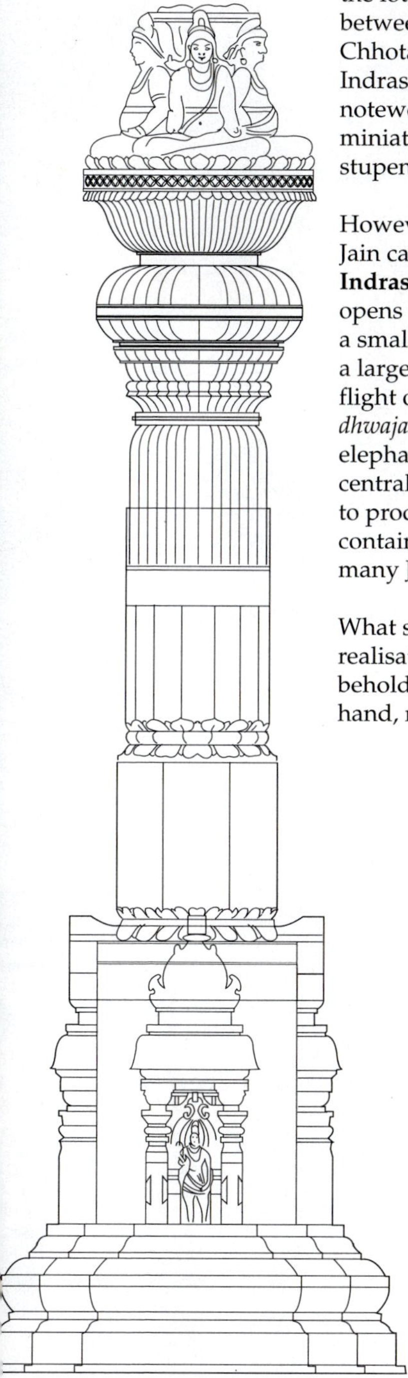

A further 2 kms along the rock-face are the Jain caves, the most recent of the lot, having been excavated between AD 800-1100. Of these the Chhota Kailasa (Cave 30) and the Indrasabha (Cave 32) are the most noteworthy. **Chhota Kailasa** is a miniaturised version of the stupendous Hindu Kailasa Temple.

However, the masterpiece of the Jain caves is the two-storeyed **Indrasabha** temple. The doorway opens onto a courtyard containing a small shrine, but the temple itself is a large edifice attained by a high flight of steps and flanked by a huge *dhwajasthamba* and a statue of an elephant. The three-sides of the central quadrangle are carved over to produce a two-storeyed facade containing a series of shrines to the many Jain *tirthankaras* or saints.

What staggers one at Ellora is the realisation that all that beauty one beholds was fashioned by human hand, more than a millenium ago.

Left:
The *dhwajasthamba* in Indrasabha cave

Below:
The goddess of prosperity adorns the first floor wall of the Indrasabha

Excursions:

Grishneshwar: This Shiva temple a kilometre away from the Ellora Caves is one of the 12 *jyotirlingas* or the *lingas* of light that are held in deep reverence by Hindus.

Khuldabad: The little town of Khuldabad, 3 kms from Ellora is held holy by Deccan Muslims. It is also the burial place of the Mughal emperor Aurangzeb, who eschewed elaborate mausoleums for a plain tomb in the compound of a Sufi saint's *dargah*.

Daulatabad: A further 13 kms down the road back to Aurangabad stands the hill fort of Daulatabad. Earlier a stronghold of the Hindu dynasty of the Yadavas and known as Devgiri, it was renamed Daulatabad in the 12th century by Sultan Mohammed bin Tughlaq, who made a futile attempt to relocate his capital from Delhi to this Deccan town.

Rising high out of a small hill whose sides had been hewn to steepness, the Daulatabad fort was said to be almost impregnable. Not only did it have three concentric circles of fortifications, it also had a series of ingenious mazes and a string of booby traps.

GETTING THERE

By Air:
Aurangabad's Chikalthana airport (30 kms away) is the nearest airport and is directly linked to Mumbai, Delhi, Jaipur and Udaipur.

By Rail:
Aurangabad is directly connected to Mumbai, Delhi, Agra and Bhopal. Alternatively, you can take a bus or taxi to Jalgaon, a mainline junction, from where you get faster express trains to Mumbai and Delhi.

By Road:
Aurangabad is connected to all major cities and towns by good trains. The Maharashtra State Road Transport Corporation runs ordinary and luxury buses from here to Mumbai (392 kms).

Left:
A series of niches carved with figures of Jain *tirthankaras* in Cave 32, the Indrasabha cave

Right:
An imposing stone elephant dominates the courtyard of the Jain temple in Cave 32

OLD GOA

Churches and Convents

Gently-swaying palms, heavy with fruit; stretches of smooth, golden sand, disturbed only by the zigzag patterns left by sandcrabs and the rhythmic crashing of frothy waves. This is what lures tourists to Goa and few of them venture beyond the beaches. But take a drive through the less-popular interiors of Goa and experience its unique cultural heritage.

The impact of 450 years of Portuguese colonial rule is apparent in every aspect of Goan life – in the food and dress, in the houses painted in gay colours and in the *joie de vivre* of the people. In every village, the fresh lime-washed facade of a church stands out like a beacon in the deep green countryside.

Se Cathedral

The Portuguese explorer Alphonso de Albuquerque captured Goa in 1510 and the Portuguese ruled the territory till its independence on 19 December 1961. The colony of Goa, with its epicentre at Goa Velha or Old Goa, became the capital of the vast eastern empire of the Portuguese, sharing the same civic privileges as Lisbon. It was often described as Goa Dourada or Golden Goa.

The early efforts of the Roman Catholic missionaries to introduce Christianity into Goa were rather half-hearted until the arrival in 1542 of the Jesuits, who were driven by the zeal of medieval crusaders. Francis Xavier, one of the founders of the Society of Jesus, better known as the Jesuits, rapidly became the patron saint of Goa.

Below:
Church and Convent of St Monica, Goa's first convent for nuns is now the Mater Dei Institute

The court in Lisbon instructed the civil administration in Goa to render maximum support to the church and huge amounts were diverted for the establishment of convents and monasteries. It is ironic that in the 17th century, even as Portuguese trade and commerce began dwindling, a grandiose effort was being made to erect more churches and cathedrals in Goa.

Church and Convent of St Cajetan: Built by the Theatines (1656-1700) the Church is shaped like the Greek cross. The monastery attached to it was rebuilt in the 18th century and is today a post-graduate theological college.

The churches in Old Goa aimed to overawe the local population into conversion and to impress upon them the superiority of the foreign religion. So, the facades were made tall and lofty and the interiors were magnificent, with twisted Bernini columns, decorated pediments, profusely-carved gilt altars and colourful wall paintings and frescoes.

Locally available laterite was used in the construction of the churches while the trimmings were sometimes of basalt. Laterite being a very porous stone, the churches had to be plastered and finished with a lime white-wash. In fact, the colour white was so identified with churches that the local administration ruled that no house could be painted that colour.

The Cross in front of the Convent and Church of St Francis of Assisi. The Church of St Francis of Assisi was built for the Franciscan friars in 1521 and then rebuilt in 1661. The church has a Tuscan facade and a Baroque interior. The interior is rib-vaulted and decorated with bold floral frescoes.

By 1635, following waves of epidemics, the seat of power moved from Old Goa to Panjim, bringing about its inevitable decline. Looking at the overgrown jungle that covers most of Old Goa, it is difficult to imagine that the city once had grand houses and crowded *bazaars* with elegant shops. All that remains are a dozen churches, convents and monasteries.

The best way to do justice to the great city of Old Goa, is to first visit the group of three big churches – the Basilica of Bom Jesus, Se Cathedral and the Church and Convent of St Francis of Assisi. The latter houses the Archaeological Museum. Thereafter, visit the Chapel of St Catherine (1510) and the ruins of the Palace of the Inquisition, before taking a walk down the quay to view the remnants of a once bustling city. Stop briefly at the Viceroy's Arch that was rebuilt in 1599.

East of the Viceroy's Arch is the Church of St Cajetan and the Gate of

The imposing facade of the Church of Our Lady of Immaculate Conception in Panjim

the Palace of Adil Shah. What was formerly Adil Shah's principal palace was used as the Viceroy's residence from 1554-1695.

To get the best hilltop view, climb the Holy Hill. Quite a few churches and convents are scattered over the hillside: the Church of Our Lady of the Rosary (1544-49) is one of the earliest churches built; the Royal Chapel of St Anthony (1543), the patron saint of Portugal; the Church and Monastery of St Augustine; the Convent of St Monica (1606, reconstructed in 1637) and the Church and Convent of St John of God (1685). Climb down the hill and turn left till you hit the highway that takes you back to the Basilica.

The 46 metre-high tower is all that remains of the Church and Monastery of St Augustine, built in 1602

Basilica of Bom Jesus

Housing the mausoleum of Saint Francis Xavier, this church is dedicated to the Infant Jesus.

It is said that the Church of St Paul that is now destroyed inspired the design of the Basilica, which in turn was modelled on the Gesu, the Jesuit headquarter in Rome. Intricately-carved basalt embellishments make it one of the richest facades in Goa. The layout follows simple Renaissance norms while the detailing and decoration is unabashedly Baroque. At the entrance, through the west-facing façade, is a bank of columns that supports the choir gallery. The confessional is finely carved and surmounted by massive eagles.

A statue of Dom Jeronimo Mascarenhas, the church's benefactor, has been prominently placed inside the Basilica. A statue of St Ignatius of Loyola, the founder of the order of the Jesuits, is placed above the elaborately-carved and gilded altar, which also has an image of the Infant Jesus. Local craftsmen who used to decorate Hindu temples were perhaps responsible for the angels depicted here – pink and décolleté.

The Florentine sculptor Giovanni Batista Foggini made the tomb of St Francis Xavier, which was endowed by the last Medici, Cosimo III, the Duke of Tuscany, in return for the pillow on which the saint's head had last rested.

The mausoleum, made of three tiers of white marble and coloured jasper, was begun in 1594 and completed in 1698. Four bronze plaques mounted on the tomb depict four pivotal scenes from St Xavier's life: him preaching in Malacca, baptising natives, escaping the wrath of the locals on Morro Island and his death on Sancian Island, near China. An exquisitely-carved stone doorway leads to the sacristy.

GETTING THERE

By Air:
Dabolim Airport is 27 kms from Panaji city centre.

By Rail:
Margao (33 kms) and Vasco Da Gama (30 kms) are the nearest railheads

By Road:
Panaji is connected by road to Bangalore (598 kms) and Mumbai (594 kms)

The sacred relics of St Francis Xavier are kept in a silver casket in the Basilica of Bom Jesus and they draw thousands of pilgrims each year

St Francis Xavier

Every December 3, on the death anniversary of Saint Francis Xavier, thousands of people flock to Old Goa to pay homage to the saint they affectionately call *Goencho Saiba* or Lord of Goa.

Born to an aristocratic family in Spain in 1506, Francis Xavier went to study for the priesthood in Paris. It was here that he met Ignatius Loyola, the son of another Basque noble. When Loyola was ordained in 1534, he along with five young priests set up the Society of Jesus and recruited Francis Xavier to this order.

By this time, the court at Lisbon was being regularly inundated by complaints of the licentiousness rampant among the Portuguese expatriates in Goa. The King turned to the Jesuits to save these souls and in 1541 Francis Xavier was despatched to stem dissolution in Goa.

Faithful records attest that within five months of landing in Goa in May 1542, Francis Xavier founded several churches and schools and even set up a university and a printing press.

Over the next few years he worked in the Malabar, in Malacca, the Spice Islands and even Japan. In 1552 he was on his way to China when he contracted dysentery on board a ship and died. It is said that his body was coated with quicklime before it was buried on the island of Sancian, but when it was exhumed some months later, it was found to be in a perfect state of preservation, the corrosive quicklime notwithstanding. The body was brought to Goa in 1554 and the Viceroy's physician corroborated the miracle of natural preservation.

But the Vatican took a long while to sanction the beatification of Francis Xavier. And while it dithered, the body of the saint-to-be was vandalised by relic hunters. The right arm was sent to the Pope in 1614, a hand was taken to Japan and a shoulder blade and all the internal organs were strewn across sundry south Asian countries. In fact, a leading Goa family, the Pereira-Braganzas of Chandor claims to have a fingernail of the saint.

St Francis Xavier was finally canonised in 1622 and today, the sacred relics of the Saint, which are kept in the Basilica of Bom Jesus, are carried in procession to the Se Cathedral for an exposition every 10 years. The next exposition is due in AD 2004.

Se Cathedral

The Portuguese Viceroy Redondo (1561-64) was instructed by the Portuguese government to commission 'a grandiose church worthy of the wealth, power and fame of the Portuguese'. This Cathedral, built over eighty long years, is the largest in Asia and is also the seat of the archdiocese of Goa.

The Grand High Altar at Se Cathedral dedicated to St. Catherine of Alexandria

The west-facing cathedral has a Tuscan exterior with square towers flanking the 30.3 metre-high facade. One surviving tower houses the largest bell in Asia. This 17th century bell has a rather hoary past. It tolled during the infamous Inquisition to announce the start of the gruesome *auto da fe* or Acts of Faith, when suspected heretics were dragged out of the Palace of Inquisition's dungeons across the square.

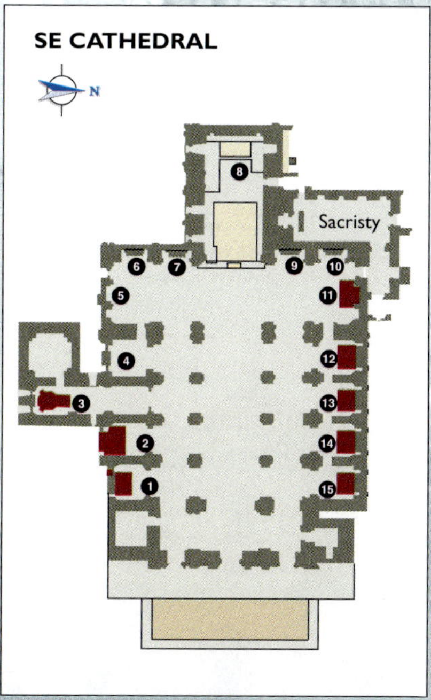

Map not to scale

1. Chapel of Our Lady of Virtues
2. Chapel of St Sebastian
3. Chapel of the Blessed Sacrament
4. Chapel of Our Lady of Life
5. Altar of Our Lady of Sorrows
6. Altar of Our Lady of Three Necessities
7. Altar of Our Lady of Hope
8. Main Altar
9. Altar of St Peter
10. Chapel of St Doloures
11. Altar of St Anne
12. Chapel of the Holy Ghost
13. Chapel of the Cross of Miracles
14. Chapel of St Bernard
15. Chapel of St Anthony

One of the fifteen side altars of Se Cathedral with elaborate filigree screens and carvings

The intricately-detailed Corinthian interior has huge pillars dividing the 76.2 metre-long central space from the side aisles. The Cathedral has as many as 15 altars and a grand altar dedicated to St Catherine of Alexandria. The gilded, ornate main altar has nine carved frames and a magnificent crucifix. The life of St Catherine of Alexandria is depicted on the panels.

Of the Cathedral's eight chapels, the chapels of the Blessed Sacrament and the Cross of Miracles have exquisite filigree work on the screens. The Cross was originally in a village church till a vision of Christ is said to have appeared on it. It is now in a box with a little hole to allow pilgrims to touch it. The relics of the blessed Martyrs of Cuncolim, who were executed trying to convert the Muslim court of the Mughal emperor Akbar, are housed in the altar of St Anne.

Se Cathedral (1562-1619) is the largest church in Asia

PATTADAKAL

The Queens' Tribute

Drive through the northern part of Deccan plateau, past miles and miles of sunflower and cotton fields, and it seems that the countryside has changed little since ancient times when the area was known as Karnata Desa or the Land of the Black Earth.

Tucked away in the interior of a state today known as Karnataka, is a dramatic gorge between two sandstone hills. Here lies Badami, the heart of the Chalukyan kingdom that ruled the Deccan between the 4th and 8th centuries AD. Badami, along with the other Chalukyan settlements of Aihole and Pattadakal forms a triangular circuit whose architectural fame attracts visitors from India and abroad.

Mallikarjuna Temple

The Chalukyas emerged as a major power after shaking off the yoke of their overlords, the Kadambas, in 6th century. Under great kings like Kirtivarman and Pulakeshin II, the Chalukyan domain was considerably enlarged. Harshvardhana, the ruler of Kannauj and one of the greatest emperors of ancient India, tried to invade the Chalukyan kingdom in AD 641 but was strongly rebuffed by Pulakeshin II.

The high point of Chalukyan rule was undoubtedly the reign of Vikramaditya II (AD 733 -746),

In Pattadakal, temples of the northern Nagara style stand beside Dravida style temples. Of the ten Chalukyan temples at this site, only four are of the northern style

1. Booking Office
2. Kadasiddhesvara
3. Galaganatha
4. Jambulinga
5. Sangamesvara
6. Column Inscription
7. Virupaksha
8. Kasivisvanatha
9. Mallikarjuna

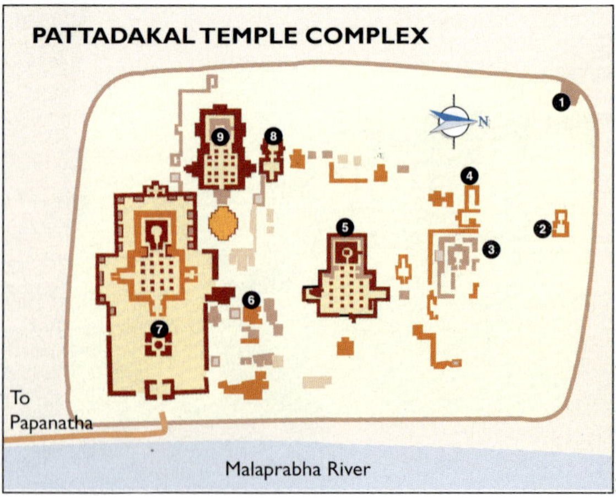

whose territorial conquests were matched only by his brilliant architectural creations. The temples of Pattadakal, to this day, bear testimony to the vigour and creativity of the Chalukyas, who have earned themselves a place in history as discerning patrons of art and architecture.

Pattadakal, a corruption of Pattada-Kisuvolal meaning Stone of Coronation, was the temple town on the banks of the Malaprabha river where the Chalukyan kings came to be crowned. The site is known to have been inhabited since prehistoric times. Ptolemy, the famous geographer (c. AD 150) refers to the place as Petrigal in his writings.

The ten main temples here live up to the Chalukyan reputation for eclecticism. It was here that we see the blending of the northern Indian Nagara and the southern Indian Dravida styles of architecture. Situated on the trading crossroads of the subcontinent, the Pattadakal architects picked up both influences and effortlessly blended them.

Mallikarjuna Temple

The Temple

Hindu temples evolved out of the modest *devagriha* or the 'house of gods' which were built beside rivers considered holy, in sacred groves and in other spots deemed hallowed.

None of these *devagrihas* have survived as they were made of non-durable materials like mud, reed, bamboo or wood, and we know of them only from references in literature. In fact, the oldest extant stone temples, including the ones at Mamallapuram, were often facsimiles of earlier wooden shrines.

A fully-evolved Nagara *shikhara* temple within the Pattadakal complex

The temple as an institution evolved in the Gupta period, around AD 350, when the sacrifice-centric Vedic religion gave way to the more personalised form of worship, the *puja*. Simultaneously, the objects of early worship, which for centuries had consisted largely of natural forces and phenomenon, gradually began to take on anthropomorphic forms. And these newly-conceived deities needed to be housed in suitable shrines.

Kalyanasundaram: **A frieze depicting the wedding of Shiva and Parvati on the walls of Virupaksha Temple**

Right:
Dancing Shiva: The exterior walls of Virupaksha Temple bear thirty five niches filled exclusively with images of Shiva

Frequent wars with the Tamil dynasty of the Pallavas – inscriptions at Pattadakal refer to them as *prakriti-amitra* or natural enemies of the early Chalukyas – led to the percolation of architectural knowledge and sculptural finesse. It is often remarked that Kailasnatha Temple at Kanchipuram strongly influenced the Virupaksha Temple at Pattadakal.

In Pattadakal, which forms the last phase of Chalukyan temple-building, you can see the shift in style from the Nagara to the Dravida form of temple building. The earlier temples like Papanatha, Jambulingesvara, Kadasiddesvara and Kasinatha represent the Nagara style, whose most prominent marker is its tapering *shikhara* or spire. The three great Shaivite temples of Sangamesvara, Virupaksha and Mallikarjuna, which collectively represent the apogee of Chalukyan architecture, are in the Dravida style, as are Galaganatha, Sunmesvara and the Jain temple outside the complex.

Virupaksha and Mallikarjuna Temples are also called Lokesvara and the Trailokesvara after the two queens of King Vikramaditya II, Lokamahadevi and Trailokamahadevi, who had the temples built to commemorate their husband's victory over the Pallavas. An inscription in Virupaksha Temple records as much. A pillar erected in AD 754 by King Kirtivarman, the son of Vikramaditya II and the younger queen, Trailokamahadevi, hails the royal patronage : '...the dear son of the glorious Vijayadityadeva who was the bruiser of

Kanchi, the glorious Vikramaditya Satyashraya…his dear queen consort …by her erected a great stone temple of the holy Lokesvara-bhattaraka. On the north of this, the younger sister of her, the glorious Lokamahadevi, a dear queen of the glorious Vikramadityadeva and the mother of the Great Kirtivarman Satyashraya… by her was erected a great stone temple of the holy Trailokesvara-bhattaraka. Thus, in the middle of these temples…there has been set up…this great stone pillar which bears the mark of the seal of the trident….'

However, as worship in Hinduism is not congregational but individual, the early temples required no more than a *square garbhagriha*, literally the 'womb-chamber', and a pillared porch. Gradually, as communities and their rituals grew, so did temple structures. A *mandapa* or hall was added for ritual dancing and banquets. For example, the hall at the Sun Temple at Konarak is referred to as *natya mandir* or *bhoga mandapa* in reference to these activites. This hall was then it was connected to the *garbhagriha* by a vestibule or *antarala*.

Over the years, a porch or *ardhamandapa* leading to the *mandapa* was added and, finally, came a *mahamandapa* or grand hall to accommodate the congregation on festivals.

Some ruins of flat-roofed Vishnu temples from the 5th century AD discovered in central India – there is one at Sanchi too – are the earliest remains of temples in India. It is in peninsular India that we can lineally trace temple architecture. These structures are also better preserved because most ancient temples are functional shrines even today.

Throughout the country, the temple sanctuary as a whole is known as the *vimana*, with its upper, pyramidal portion called the *shikhara*. The edifice almost always faces the east, to catch the first rays of the sun.

The two major styles of temple architecture in India, the Nagara school of the North and the Dravida of the South, are both variations on this basic theme.

The walls of **Virupaksha** (AD 745) and **Mallikarjuna** (AD 755) Temples abut each other, and they mirror each other's architectural features, but for the fact that the Virupaksha is more spacious and in a better state of preservation. They were probably built by architects Sarvasiddhi Achari and Anivartya Gunda, who received the highest royal honour from King Vikramaditya II for Virupaksha Temple.

Local women on the steps of the eastern gateway of Virupaksha Temple

The walls of the two temples are a showcase in stone of Shaivite imagery. They are quite clearly royal-sponsored showpieces of the wealth, both material and creative, of the Chalukyan dynasty.

Virupaksha is the biggest temple at Pattadakal and the only one with a *pratoli* or ornamental gateway.

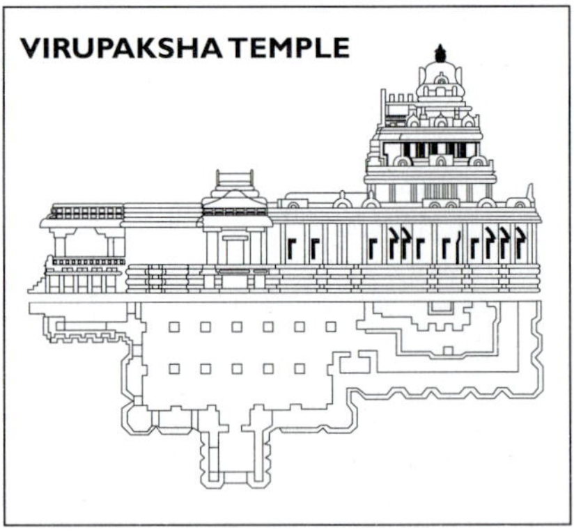

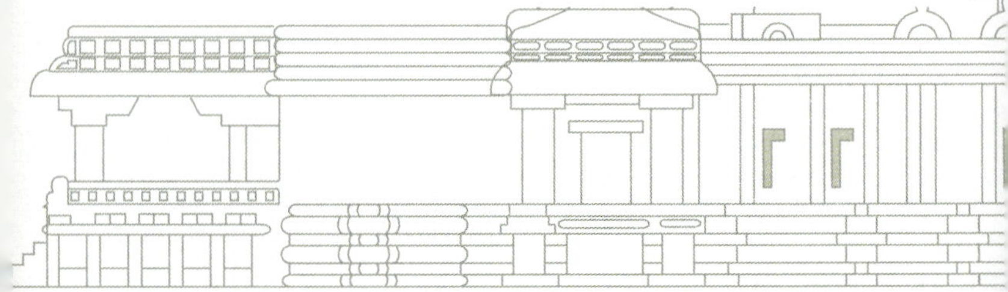

Virupaksha is also the one with the greatest influence of the southern style of temple-building. The contact, largely in the form of repeated invasions, between the Chalukyas and the Pallavas is a historical fact. And this influenced the architectural creations of both dynasties.

Behind the high walls of both Virupaksha and Mallikarjuna Temples lies a spacious *prakara* or courtyard and the *parivaralaya* or the tutelary shrines. Both temples are *chaturstala* or four-storeyed (counting the ground floor) and are *sandhara* shrines, that is, they have an ambulatory around the *garbhagriha* or the *sanctum*. And in both, the enshrined *linga* of granite makes a striking contrast to the red sandstone of the temple itself.

There is no specific geographical line for the change in style from Nagara to Dravida. There are temples in the Dravidian style as far north as Ellora and temples made according to the Nagara school as far south as Dharwar in Karnataka. In fact, the town of Pattadakal is unique in that it contains temples of both schools.

Sometime in the eighth century AD, temple-builders in the South began showing a distinct individuality in their structures. At first the differences were slight – the *shikhara* or spire that crowns the *vimana* was traditionally curvilinear in the North, but pyramidal and storeyed in the South. The large Dravida *vimana* took in the congregation, which in the North had to be accommodated in the *mahamandapa*. Pillars, capitals and mouldings all began to take on new shapes in the South.

One of the most striking architectural differences was the overwhelming presence of the *gopuram* in the temples of the mature Dravida school. These ornamental gateways rose to outsized heights and made the Dravida temple dominate the surrounding countryside.

By far the greatest difference is that the Dravida temples were much more than just centres of worship; they were autonomous communities that, over the centuries, became nucleii for urban settlements, as is the case at Thanjavur, Madurai and Srirangam. To this day, the southern temples house priests, own land and cattle, and employ hundreds of musicians, florists, cooks and artisans.

The colossal granite Nandi in its pavilion outside Virupaksha Temple

The courtyard of Virupaksha Temple is pierced on the east, north and south sides by pillared porches. Enter the compound through the east gate to find the tall, enclosing wall studded with sub-shrines for the various *parivara devatas* or family deities. These originally numbered 32 and were ranged 16 to each side.

Just inside the main gateway is a raised, pillared pavilion housing a three-metre long, black statue of Nandi, the bull vehicle of Lord Shiva. The pillars of this Nandi *mandapa* bear beautifully-carved couples, women with parasols, *ganas* and elephants.

The ceiling panel of the eastern porch of Virupaksha is a striking composition depicting Surya, the Sun god, standing on a chariot yoked to seven horses and flanked by images of Usha and Pratyusha. The exterior walls of the temple carry 35 niches, filled solely with images of Shiva. The most eye-catching among them are the Natesa and the Uma Maheshwari. What is striking about these niches are the *toranas* or ceremonial door hangings that project outwards, enhancing the effect of the image.

Right:
A sculpture on the western wall of the Nandi *mandapa* of Virupaksha Temple

FESTIVALS

- **Annual Pattadakal Dance Festival:** 4th week of January

The niches are interspersed with 18 stone windows that have floral and animal patterns imaginatively carved into *jalis* to let in light.

The interior hall is broken into aisles by four rows of pillars and these pillars and walls of the main *mandapa* make the Virupaksha particularly vibrant. Especially remarkable are the sculptural representations of scenes from the *Mahabharata*, the *Ramayana*, and the *Panchatantra* on the pillars.

The artists have captured a great sense of drama in the many figures carved inside, from the fierce guardians of the doorways or the *dwarapalas*, who always appear in pairs, to the elegant, elaborately-coiffed women draped around the inside pilasters.

Virupaksha also has subsidiary shrines to Ganesha and Mahishasuramardini, and the latter is among the most striking sculptures at Pattadakal.

Left:
A sculpted niche in Papanatha Temple

Below:
Frieze from the walls of Virupaksha Temple

Towering over the *garbhagriha* in both Virupaksha and Mallikarjuna Temples is the *vimana* whose clearly defined pyramidal form reveals a pleasing symmetry. Both are heavily ornamented with miniature temples and *hamsamalas* or swan-linked garlands. This feature exists in a more experimental form in the earlier Sangamesvara Temple.

Another attractive feature common to both temples is the *torana* or the entrance of the *garbhagriha* and the statues of *mithuna* or loving couples that adorn it.

Papanatha Temple (c. AD 680) is a rather squat building with bulky pillars and earthy decorations. Some art historians have also suggested that Papanatha, with its Nagara *shikhara,* was originally dedicated to the worship of Vishnu and Surya.

Below:
A loving couple on a porch pillar in Mallikarjuna Temple

But when the Chalukyas switched from Vaishnavism to Shaivism, the temple too switched deities.

The Chalukyan temples at Pattadakal, particularly Virupaksha, embody a great phase of architecture and were a definite influence on later temples, especially the colossal Kailasa Temple at Ellora.

MUSEUM

The Archaeological Survey of India has a museum in Badami.

Timing:
Closed Fridays

Excursions

Aihole was the regional capital of the Chalukyas and has around 70 structures of which a few are striking. Ladkhan Temple is the earliest and reveals the post-Gupta influence in its simple doorways. Durga Temple is an interesting temple as it has a round aspidal *sanctum* that reveals Buddhist influences. By far the most advanced in terms of layout is Huchimallagudi Temple. This temple has a passage leading to a pillared *mandapa,* as well as a porch, displaying the methods and techniques of succeeding styles.

Durga Temple at Aihole

Some 29 kms from Pattadakal, **Badami** is also the base from which to travel to Pattadakal and Aihole (46 kms), as well as being the place to stay in. The cave temples of Badami are situated in a red sandstone cliff and are dedicated to Vishnu and Shiva. There are also some Jain caves. This is the formative period of Chalukyan architecture.

On the streets of Badami town

Cave 4 in Badami:
A Jain cave built by King
Pulakeshin II

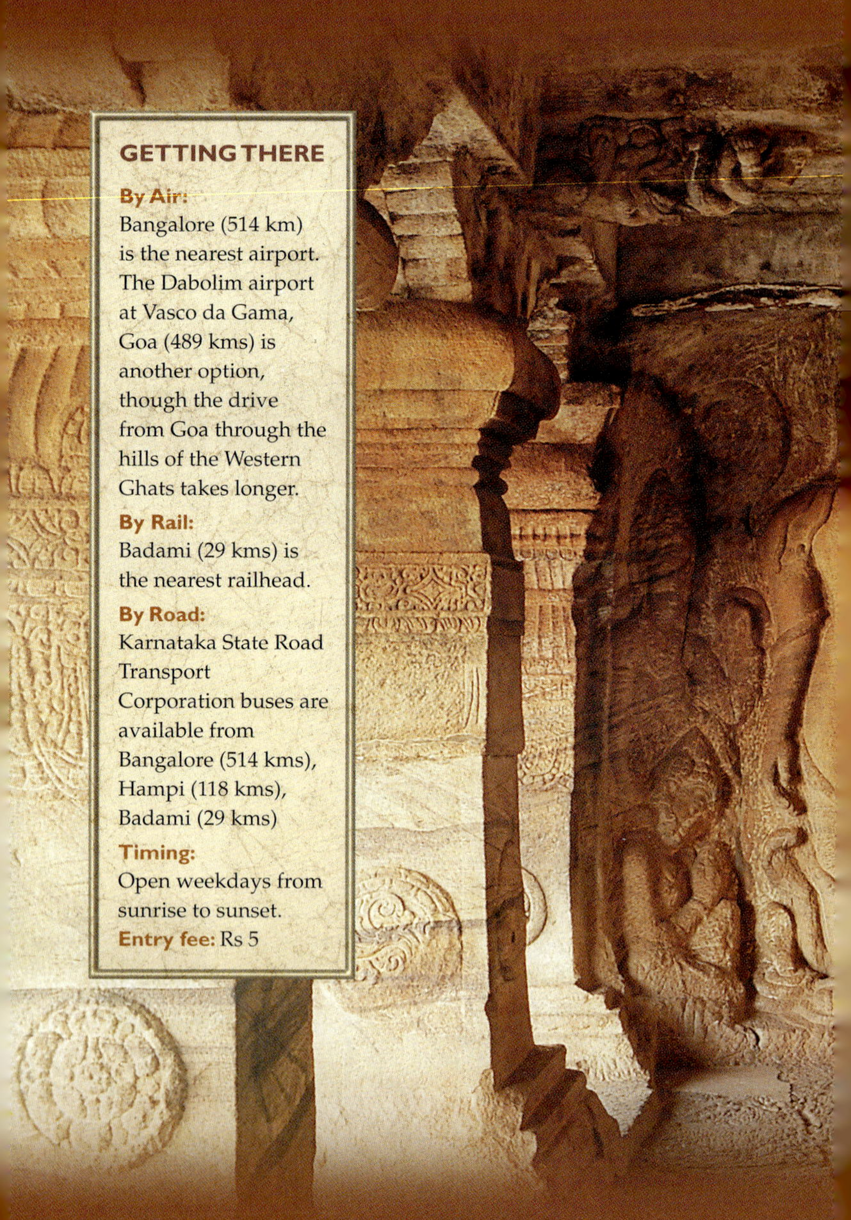

GETTING THERE

By Air:
Bangalore (514 km) is the nearest airport. The Dabolim airport at Vasco da Gama, Goa (489 kms) is another option, though the drive from Goa through the hills of the Western Ghats takes longer.

By Rail:
Badami (29 kms) is the nearest railhead.

By Road:
Karnataka State Road Transport Corporation buses are available from Bangalore (514 kms), Hampi (118 kms), Badami (29 kms)

Timing:
Open weekdays from sunrise to sunset.

Entry fee: Rs 5

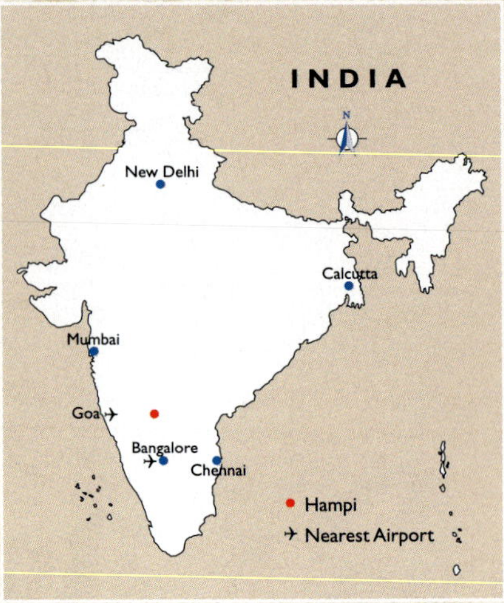

HAMPI

The Magnificent City of Victory

Hills of bare rock rise beside the swift Tungabhadra river as it swirls and curves through a barren landscape strewn with giant granite boulders. In this daunting terrain, many centuries ago, rose a magnificent medieval city that rivalled the most famous cities of the world – the imperial Vijayanagar or 'the City of Victory'.

Once the Vijayanagar empire dominated the land south of the Tungabhadra river. Its capital city, of the same name, was envied for its rich *bazaars*, crowded temples and fabulous palaces. Merchants and ambassadors from faraway lands came to its royal court looking for trade and alliances.

The stone chariot in the Vitthala Temple compound

In the 14th century when large parts of northern India were already under Muslim rule, this region was part of the Hindu kingdom of Kampili. In 1326, the army of the ruler of Delhi, Mohammed bin Tughlaq defeated and killed the king of Kampili. Among those taken prisoner were two brothers, Harihara and Bukka, both treasury officers of Kampili, who were forced to convert to Islam. Some years later, the Sultan sent the brothers back to govern the province. In 1336 they laid the foundation of an independent kingdom, denied any allegiance to the Tughlaqs and became Hindus once again.

Far right:
A detail from the Mahanavami Dibba

Below:
An ornate pillar, typical to Vijayanagar, in which the pillar shaft becomes the core of a huge sculpture. The most conspicuous part of the imagery often is a rearing horse.

They laid the foundation of the Sangama dynasty with its citadel in Vijayanagar. The original name of the city was probably Vidyanagar after the great Hindu sage, Vidyaranya.

The greatest monarch of Vijayanagar was Krishna Deva Raya who reigned from 1509 to 1529. Travellers from Arabia and Italy came to his court and he had cordial diplomatic relations with the Portuguese at Goa. A scholar and poet, he was an enlightened and secular king. Krishna Deva Raya built some of the finest palaces and temples in Vijayanagar.

Many travellers have chronicled the magnificence of Vijayanagar. The Portuguese traveller Fernao Nuniz wrote, 'What I saw… seemed as large as Rome, and very beautiful to the sight…' while the Arab Abdur Razzaq felt that the beauty of Vijayanagar was such 'that the pupil of the eye has never seen such a place'.

For two centuries, until its disastrous defeat in 1565 by the combined armies of Bijapur, Golconda and Ahmednagar, Vijayanagar dominated the region. Thereafter, the city was abandoned and occupied by invaders who robbed and pillaged it, massacring its people and systematically destroying its buildings. Vijayanagar was left desolate, its pavilions and temples standing forgotten among palm trees and rice fields. It would be found in the early years of the 20th century – an amazing medieval city frozen in time, its ruins telling stories in stone of kings and warriors, temple dancers and merchants.

MUSEUM

Excellent Archaeological Survey of India Museum at Kamalapuram. Good collection of sculptures and scale model of Hampi.

Entry fee: Rs 5

Timing:
10 am to 5pm
Closed on Friday

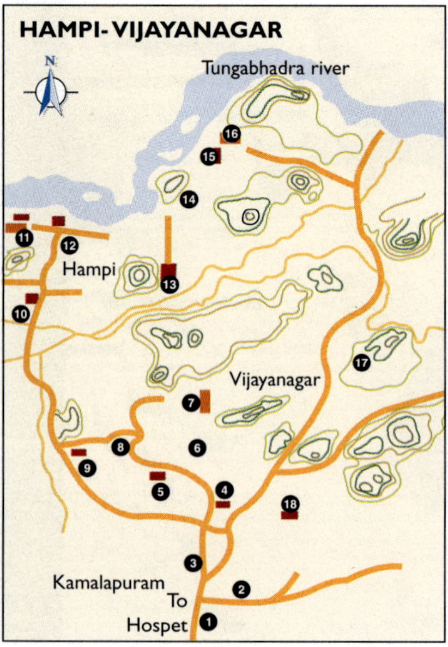

Map not to scale

1. Nageshwara Temple
2. Archaeological Museum
3. Archaeological Survey Office
4. Queen's Bath
5. Mahanavami Dibba
6. Lotus Mahal Restaurant
7. Lotus Mahal
8. Hazara Rama Temple
9. Prasanna Virupaksha Temple
10. Krishna Temple
11. Virupaksha Temple
12. Ganesh Temple
13. Tiruvengalanatha Temple
14. Narasimha Temple
15. King's Balance
16. Vitthala Temple
17. Raghunatha Temple
18. Bhima's Gate

Robert Sewell, the British civil servant who discovered the ruins of Vijayanagar, wrote of its tragic end, 'Never perhaps in the history of the world has such havoc been wrought, and wrought suddenly, on so splendid a city'.

Today the monuments of the imperial city lie within the villages of Hampi and Kamalapuram in Bellary district of Karnataka, 353 kms from the nearest airport at Bangalore. The monuments are spread over 26 square kms and include a citadel area, a temple area, *bazaars*, fortifications, river landings and gateways.

The sculpture and architecture of Vijayanagar are noted for the elegance of design and intricate carvings. The local stone, granite and a green chlorite, were easily available and used with great imagination in buildings and free-standing sculptures.

Elaborate figure sculptures adorn the walls of the Hampi monuments

Exquisite pillars in the *mahamandapa* of the Vitthala Temple

Royal Enclosure

The Royal Enclosure or the Citadel area has the royal buildings that include audience halls, palaces, pavilions, public baths, stables and guard quarters. However these are in a much more ruined state than the temples.

The city also had massive fortifications, the walls interspersed by gateways high enough to allow an elephant to pass. Bastions and watchtowers were built high on the hills and there are remains of a bridge across the Tungabhadra.

Entering the royal enclosure by the road past the **Queen's Bath**, one passes a number of vast stone platforms. The largest is the Throne Platform, also called **Mahanavami Dibba**, from where the king inaugurated the *Navaratri*

Above:
Lotus Mahal: The ceiling of the two-storeyed pavilion in the *zenana* or women's enclosure is a series of vaults and domes

Below:
The recently excavated Pushkarini Pool with geometrically patterned steps in green chlorite

celebrations. The 12 metre-high granite platform is covered with carved friezes that depict the pageantry of parades – marching troops, horses, elephants, camels, dancers, musicians, clowns and foreign envoys in exotic clothes.

Nuniz describing a *Mahanavami* celebration writes, '...then came thirty six of the most beautiful of the king's wives covered with gold and pearls, and in the hand of each, a vessel of gold with a lamp of oil burning in it.'

Right:
A detail from Mahanavami Dibba or the throne platform from which the king reviewed his troops

Just behind the Dibba are remains of a stone aqueduct which show that there was an elaborate system of channels laid out to provide water to the Citadel. Nearby is the recently excavated tank, the **Pushkarini Pool**.

Before reaching the Citadel lies the **Queen's Bath**. The plain exterior belies the delightfully ornate interiors. An elegant corridor with projecting balconies and arched niches surrounds the square bath.

Hazara Rama Temple was probably the royal chapel. Its name means a Thousand Ramas, though scholars speculate that it could also be a variation of the Telegu word *hajaramu* which means entrance of a palace.

Close to the Lotus Mahal is the **Elephant Stables**, with eleven large stalls domed in different styles.

The Temple Area

The temples in Vijayanagar, the Virupaksha, the Vitthala and the Krishna, are laid out in the traditional style of South Indian temples. The main shrine or *garbhagriha* has a circumambulation path, the *pradakshina prakara*. The complex is enclosed by a wall with soaring gateways or *gopurams*. The flat roof of the shrine has a brick and plaster pinnacle, the *shikhara*. There are other pavilions within the courtyard, the most important being the Amman shrine for the consort goddess of the deity. The most decorative pavilion is the *kalyana mandapa* where once a year the deity is married to his consort. It is the largest temple in Hampi with a number of subsidiary shrines within a large walled courtyard. The giant 52 metre-high *gopuram* dominates the landscape.

Below:
The shrine to Goddess Pampa at the Virupaksha Temple: Virupaksha is also known as Pampapati or Lord of Pampa, the daughter of Brahma. The Tungabhadra river is also known as Pampanadi

Above left:
A detail from the *gopuram* of the Virupaksha Temple

Facing page:
The massive *gopuram* of the Virupaksha Temple facing Hampi Bazaar

The Hampi Bazaar is a wide road, that could once accommodate four chariots running abreast and had a row of two-storeyed colonnaded structures. Today there are curio shops and telephone booths, even a cyber café in what was once a great *bazaar.*

Matanga and Hemkuta hills flank Hampi Bazaar. There are a group of picturesque temples on the slopes of the Hemkuta hill. Dating from the 9th to the 14th century, these are built in the early Vijayanagar style with stone pyramidal roofs. On the road outside the Virupaksha Temple stand two wooden temple cars or *rathas* which are taken out once a year for the car festival. Looking down from Matanga Hill, you can see the **Achyut Raya Temple**, framed like a painting by the palm trees, paddy fields and the silver gleam of the Tungabhadra.

The finest temple in Hampi is the jewel-like **Vitthala Temple** built by Krishna Deva Raya, and dedicated to Lord Vishnu as Vitthala.

A gorgeously decorated *maha mandapa*, an open pavilion with 56 intricately-carved pillars, is attached to the main *sanctum*. There are pillars in a composite design of slender columnettes that Percy Brown describes as, 'miniature pillars, slender, mystical and dreamy, like gothic nook-shafts'.

The ceiling of the *kalyana mandapa* is carved in lotus designs and still carry patches of bright colours that once covered these buildings. The *ratha*, a stone chariot standing before the *maha mandapa*, is a perfect stone replica of a wooden chariot and so finely carved that the wheels actually rotate.

A short walk from the Vitthala Temple is the stone frame called the **King's Balance**. Weighing scales were attached to it for the ceremony of weighing the king in coins and gems on auspicious occasions.

FESTIVALS

- **Virupaksha Car Festival** – January-February
- **Purandara Dasa**
- **Aradhana Music Festival** – January-February
- **Vijayanagar Festival** – December

The *ratha* or stone chariot in the compound of the Vitthala Temple houses an image of the divine bird, Garuda

The colossal free-standing figure of **Narasimha** has become a visual symbol of Vijayanagar. Even in its damaged state it is an awesome sight, looming over the paddy fields with ferocious power. The monolithic rock figure stands 6.7 metres high. Originally it was a four armed figure of Narasimha, the man-lion incarnation of Vishnu, with the goddess Lakshmi perched on one thigh and a seven-hooded Naga, the snake god, curved protectively over his head.

The monolithic image of Narasimha was one of the last additions to Vijayanagar by Krishna Deva Raya

GETTING THERE

By Air:
Bangalore (353 kms), Goa (323 kms) are the nearest airports

By Rail:
Hospet (13 kms), linked daily to Bangalore is the best option

By Road:
From Bangalore, KSRTC buses run daily to Hospet. Buses, cars, autorickshaws available at Hospet.

Also worth visiting are the giant Ganesha statues on the road to Hampi Bazaar. Affectionately called Sasivekalu or Mustard Seed, and Kadalekalu or a Grain of Gram, they watch over Hampi with benign majesty. Near the Ganeshas is the **Krishna Temple** built by Krishna Deva Raya with interesting carvings on the pillars and the avatars of Vishnu depicted on the gateway.

Above left:
Shiva Temple: Next to the Narasimha statue is a small single-chambered temple containing an enormous *linga*, over 3 metres high, with its base permanently in water.

Krishna Temple with the three-storeyed *vimana* in the background

BRIHADISVARA

Chola Tribute to Lord Shiva

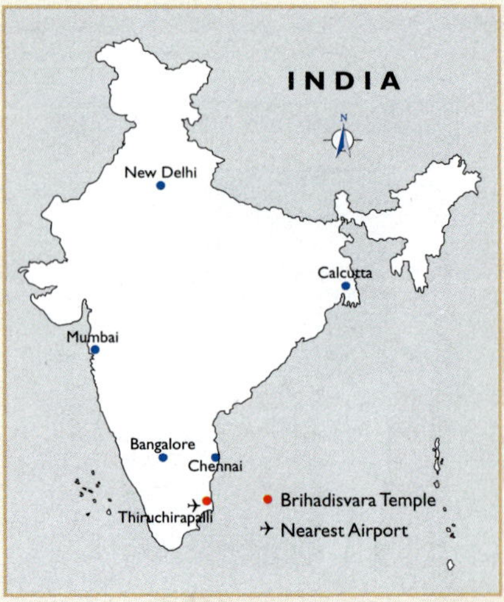

The most enduring aspect of the four-century rule of the Cholas (AD 850-AD 1280) was the extensive temple-building they undertook, creating a sacred circuit of 108 Shiva temples in the Kaveri delta.

Under Rajakesari Rajaraja who came to the throne in AD 985, and his son Rajendra I, the Cholas expanded their territories to cover the entire peninsula. As they went further, conquering the Maldive Islands, Sri Lanka, parts of Malaysia, and moving upwards to touch the river Ganga, their kingdom prospered.

Brihadisvara Temple

As long as the moon-crested deity (Shiva) sports with his consort on the Kailasa mountain, as long as Hari (Vishnu) performs meditative sleep on the serpent couch...so long may the Chola family protect from danger the circle of the whole earth.

– A Chola stone inscription

A devout Shiva *bhakta*, Rajaraja – as also his son – gave thanks to the Lord by erecting grand temples. Soon, the landscape of Tamil Nadu was punctuated with lofty spires or *shikharas* and magnificent temple gateways or *gopurams*.

At the heart of the Chola power structure, in the wondrous city of Thanjavur, Rajaraja erected his *magnum opus*, the Rajarajesvaram-udayar. It was built as a tribute to his patron deity Shiva and also in expiation for the bloodshed he had caused in numerous wars.

The temple was consecrated in AD 1010, on the 275th day of the 25th regnal year of Rajaraja's reign, and it lives on, with all rituals and festivals duly conducted. The only thing that has changed is its name: during the rule of the Nayakas, who succeeded the Cholas, it was called Periya Udayar Koil, whose Sanskritised version is Brihadisvara. Today the locals call it just Periya Koil or the Big Temple.

Work on Brihadisvara began in AD 1003. The area around Thanjavur is fertile flatlands. The nearest rocky areas are around Thiruchirapalli, many miles away, from where the granite for the massive temple was probably quarried.

Left:
Through the main gate

Right:
A *gana* on the outer wall of the main shrine holding up the outlet for the water poured on the *linga*

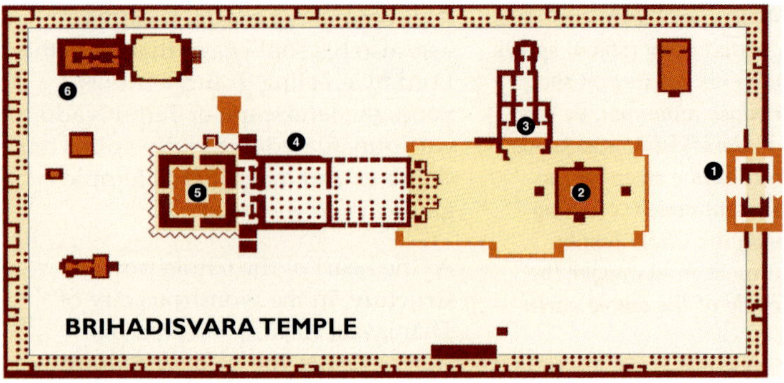

1. The second *gopuram*
2. Nandi *mandapa*
3. Amman shrine
4. *Mandapa*
5. *Garbhagriha*
6. Subrahmanya shrine

Slowly, the temple rose to tower over the countryside. Seven years later, the *shikhara* was ready, awaiting only the *uttamavimana*. Legend has it that a ramp of packed earth was constructed, beginning 6.4 kms away in the village of Sarapallam. The incline spanned the distance to reach the temple and elephants pulled the 81-tonne granite block mounted on logs to the top of the *shikhara*.

Brihadisvara is the showpiece of Chola architecture. The two elaborately carved *gopurams*, widely separated from each other, lead the devotee to the huge 152 metres by 76 metres inner courtyard. Just ahead stands the monolithic granite statue of Nandi, Shiva's vehicle, ensconced under a painted canopy of the later Nayaka period.

The courtyard itself is encircled by a massive granite wall, which has 1008 Nandi statues on it. There are cloisters on three sides of this vast courtyard and the ones to the left house 108 Shiva *lingas* of different shapes and sizes.

Beyond is the central shrine, whose *garbhagriha* enshrines a massive 3.6 metre-high *linga,* striking in its simplicity. The huge black granite *linga* is also called the *adavallan* or One-who-dances-well.

The *garbhagriha* has a *sandhara nali* or circumambulatory path between its inner and outer walls, allowing devotees to circle the shrine in a clockwise direction.

A colossal *dwarapala* flanking the side entrance to the Brihadisvara shrine

Below:
Nandi *mandapa*

The beautifully sculpted inner facade of the second *gopuram*

The east entrance to the Brihadisvara Temple leading up to the pillared *mandapa*

The passage around the *garbhagriha* is closed to the public and special permission from the Archaeological Survey of India is needed to enter it to view the few original Chola murals that survive. Unfortunately, most were painted over by the later rulers. Worth viewing is a line drawing showing Rajaraja and his mentor, the Shaivite saint Karuvur Devar.

There is a another circumambulatory gallery on the first floor which is popularly called the Bharatnatyam Gallery because it contains statues of Shiva in the various dance poses described in the ancient dance treatise, the *Natyashastra*. Some 108 figures were planned, but only 79 were completed – in fact the 80th figure is left half-done – because the then king, Rajendra I, acquired a new centre of attention, the other Brihadisvara temple in his new capital Gangaikondacholapuram.

The greatest attraction of the Thanjavur temple is its magnificent *srivimana*, that rises to a height of 66.8 metres from the base and is divided into 13 *talas* or storeys. The square chamber of the *garbhagriha* gives way to an octagonal hollow half-way up the spire for maximum load leverage. It is crowned by an 81-tonne block of granite called the *uttamavimana*, on which rests a gold-covered *kalasha* or finial, 3.6 metres high.

What makes this *vimana* unique is the almost microscopic adherence to measurements – and this in an age when precision tools were unknown. The *vimana* is exactly eight times the width of the *garbhagriha* so that the load could be properly distributed. And the main Shiva *linga*, Nandi and the *uttamavimana* are all exactly 3.6 metres high.

The temple's wealth

The Brihadisvara was probably the richest temple of its time. Unlike most other temples of South India, including the ones at Srirangam and Chidambaram, its endowment had not accrued over centuries but was the result of one lavish grant from Rajaraja Chola of 38,000 *kalanju* units of gold amassed from his wars with Kerala, Madurai and Sri Lanka.

According to detailed inscriptions on the temple walls, this was apart from jewellery gifted for the idols, the revenue of many villages, as well as vast tracts of land and herds of cattle, whose produce alone would fund the food, flowers and even unguents required for the worship of the gods over coming centuries. Individual donors, too, deposited sums of money with *brahmins* of the town, who invested the money and passed on the interest to the temple.

The *brahmins* who managed this wealth proved to have a sound grasp of worldly finance – the temple not only funded commercial enterprises, but also acted as banker and money-lender.

The Brihadisvara drew its vast personnel from other shrines in the Kaveri delta. These temples not only seconded numerous priests, watchmen, musicians and *devadasis* or dancing girls to the Brihadisvara, but also paid their stipends.

Little wonder, then, that the Brihadisvara Temple's original employment roll included 400 *devadasis*, 212 attendants, 57 musicians and chanters of texts, apart from hundreds of priests.

Queen Sujan Bai from a 19th-century mural in the Subrahmanya shrine within Brihadisvara complex

Chandeswara shrine is the oldest sub-shrine in the complex

The famed Chola sculptures in the temple niches display a marked elegance, while the massive stone *dwarapalas* or gatekeepers at the major entrances are striking in their ability to convey a sense of brute strength.

The courtyard houses shrines for Parvati, Subrahmanya and Ganesha that were added later during the reign of the Nayakas. The Subrahmanya shrine has exquisite carvings and some fine paintings. Of the minor shrines, the Chandeshwara is the oldest and all temple accounts were carried out in the name of this deity during the Chola period.

The temple rituals have changed little in the thousand years of its existence. Even today, the deity is woken up to the accompaniment of ritual music and, after a morning bath, the rituals start with the Vedic chants and singing. In time-honoured tradition, the temple is closed in the afternoon to allow the Lord a nap and the priests return to their homes in adjoining streets, where their families have lived since the time of Rajaraja Chola. At four in the evening, the temple doors are opened again and the rituals start until it is time for the Lord to retire for the night.

FESTIVALS

- **The Thyagaraja Arathanai Music festival** at Thiruvaiyaru in honour of the great saint Thyagaraja, held from 11-14 January every year.
- **Mahamaham** held once every 12 years during February - March.
  Last held in 1992.
- **Arulmigu Thyagaraja Samy Temple Car Festival** – at Tiruvarur every March/April.
- **Muthupallaku Thiruvizha** held in Thanjavur every March/April.
- **A festival of dance and music** is held in the Brihadisvara Temple every 2nd and 4th Saturday by the South Zone Cultural Centre.

GETTING THERE

By Air:
Thiruchirapalli (54 kms) for domestic flights and Chennai Airport (334 kms) for international flights are the nearest airports.

By Rail:
Thanjavur Railway Station is 8 kms away from the Brihadisvara Temple. Thiruchirapalli is the nearest junction.

By Road:
The Thiruvalluvar Transport Corporation and the Rajiv Gandhi Transport Corporation run buses to all major cities of the South from the main bus-stand at Thiruchirapalli.

Excursions

Darasuram (36 kms) is a must-see for the Airatesvara Temple. Fashioned in the mould of a chariot, this temple showcases the mastery of the Chola sculptors in the beautiful animal carvings on its balustrade.

Kumbakonam (36 kms) is an ancient town with great temples like the 17th-century Adikumbeswarar Temple, the imposing Ramasamy Temple with its massive Chola sculptures and the 9th-century Nageswaram Temple with its stucco horses. Kumbakonam is a shopper's delight for those interested in handloom cloth and other curios.

Thiruchirapalli (54 kms) is famous for its Rock Fort, built around 1660. It is also the base for a trip to the temple town of **Srirangam**, 13 kms away. Standing on an island in the Kaveri, the focus of Srirangam town is the Sri Ranganathaswami Temple, dedicated to Vishnu and famed for its 21 *gopurams* and collection of temple jewellery.

THE PALACE COMPLEX

The Thanjavur Palace Complex is worth a day's sightseeing. It houses the **Palace Temple** built partly by the Nayakas around AD 1515 as well as the famous **Maratha Art Gallery.**

Timing:
9 am to 1 pm on weekdays

Entry Fee:
Adults Rs 3, children Re 1
Phone: 22823

- **Royal Museum** located in the Palace complex:

Timing:
9 am to 1 pm

Entry Fee:
Adults Re 1, children 50 paise.
Phone: 31486

- **Hall of Music** is in the Royal Palace as is the **Saraswati Mahal Library** which has more than 10,000 palm-leaf manuscripts.

Other places worth seeing in the city include the Sivaganga tank near the Palace, the Tamil University and the Raja Rani Mani Mandapam.

An exquisite Chola bronze statue from the Maratha Art Gallery in the Palace Complex

MAMALLAPURAM

Sculptures in the Sand

Straddling the mouth of the Palar river, the sleepy town of Mamallapuram served the Pallava dynasty (AD 600-900) as its most important port on the Coromandel coast. It was from here that ships laden with spices and silks sailed across the Bay of Bengal to the islands of Java, Sumatra and to Cambodia.

Little wonder, then, that the Pallava kings chose this town to record their might in stone. The amazing pavilions and temples on the edge of the sea have withstood fourteen centuries of buffeting by the relentless elements, to be hailed as prototypes of Dravidian architecture.

The Shore Temple

Today, Mamallapuram is a quiet hamlet in the district of Chengalpet in Tamil Nadu. Also known as Mahabalipuram (legend has it that Lord Vishnu vanquished the giant Mahabali here), Mallapuram and Mahamalaipuram, it is 58 kms from Chennai and 72 kms from Pondicherry.

Even today, the town resounds to the sculptor's hammer. Encouraged by the government, the local stone-cutters are continuing with a craft that first flourished here fifteen hundred years ago. In fact, the government has also set up a College of Sculpture here.

The Pallavas were the first major Tamil dynasty that ruled the region that is now Tamil Nadu between the 6th and 9th century AD. The area was then called Tondainadu.

The *rathas* are stone-hewn shrines shaped as temple chariots. They continue to mystify visitors because they are obviously copies of wooden structures.

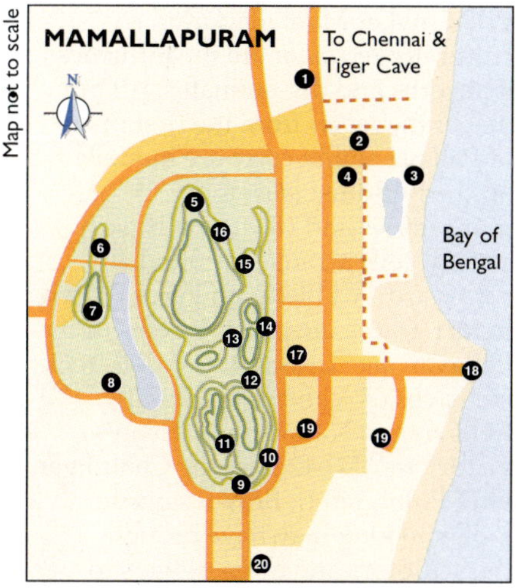

1. Mukunda Nayanar Temple
2. Post Office
3. Holiday Home
4. Tourist Office
5. Kodikal Mandapam
6. Pidari Ratha
7. Valayan Kuttal Ratha
8. PWD Bungallow
9. Dharmaraja Mandapam
10. Mahishasuramardini Cave
11. Light House
12. Krishna Mandapam
13. Varaha Mandapam
14. Arjuna's Penance
15. Ganesha Ratha
16. Krishna's Butterball
17. Archaeological Museum
18. Shore Temple
19. Youth Hostel & Camping Site
20. Five Rathas

The greatest Pallava king was Narasimhavarman (AD 640-668), fondly known as *mamalla* or little wrestler, who transformed a little seaside village into a bustling port and gave it its name.

The row of Nandi bulls on the outer wall of the Shore Temple

The temples of Mamallapuram, built largely during the reigns of Narasimhavarman and his successor Rajasimhavarman, showcases the movement from rock-cut architecture to structural building. The *mandapas* or pavilions and the *rathas* or shrines shaped as temple chariots are hewn from the granite rock face, while the famed Shore Temple, erected half a century later, is built from dressed stone.

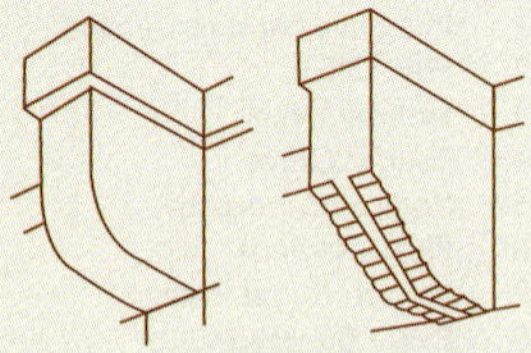

Pallava: 7th and 8th century AD

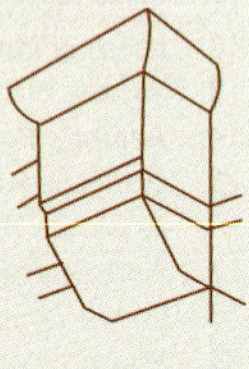

Chola: 11th century AD

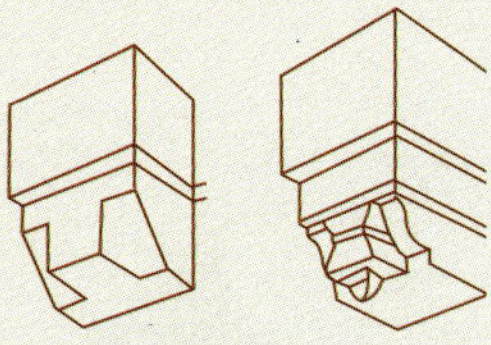

Pandya: 13th century AD

What makes Mamallapuram so culturally resonant are the influences it absorbs and disseminates. All but one of the *rathas* from the first phase of Pallava architecture are modelled on the Buddhist *viharas* or monasteries and *chaitya* halls with several cells arranged around a courtyard. Art historian Percy Brown, in fact, traces the possible roots of the Pallavan *mandapas* to the similar rock-cut caves of Ajanta and Ellora. Referring to Narasimhavarman's victory in AD 642 over the Chalukyan king Pulakesin II, Brown says the Pallavan king may have brought the sculptors and artisans back to Kanchi and Mamallapuram as 'spoils of war'.

And when the Chalukyans regained their kingdom, these workmen returned bearing memories of their work in the south with them. The similarities between Arjuna's Penance and Cave XXIV at Ajanta are particularly striking.

Some of Mamallapuram's other indigenous motifs, like the lion pilasters, the profuse decorations and precise figure sculptures and the nascent *gopuram* or gateway, in turn became *leitmotifs* of the southern style of temple building. Mamallapuram's influence can also be seen further afield in the Khmer sculptures of Angkor Thom and Angkor Vat in Cambodia and in the bas-reliefs at the Borobudur temple in Indonesia.

Of the secular architecture at Mamallapuram, the most fascinating is its elaborate water system. Little, however, remains of the non-religious buildings indicating that secular structures were probably made from less durable materials like brick and wood.

MUSEUM

Small museum on Raja Street with a good collection of granite sculptures.

Entry fee: Rs 5

Free on Fridays

The Shore Temple: Buffeted by monsoon rains and the drifting sands for over a thousand years, its twin *shikharas* still stand tall and proud, a memorial to the architectural brilliance of Pallava craftsmen.

Shore Temple

Perched on a rocky outcrop, it presides over the shoreline, serving, as Percy Brown puts it, 'a landmark by day and a beacon by night'. Designed to catch the first rays of the rising sun and to illuminate the waters after dark, the temple ended up with an unusual lay-out. As the main shrine faces the sea on the east, the gateway, the forecourt and the assembly hall of the Shore Temple all lie behind the *sanctum*.

Unusual, too, is the fact that the temple has shrines to both Shiva and Vishnu. The main *sanctum* and one of the two lesser ones on the west are dedicated to Shiva. The enclosing wall has a series of Nandi bulls on it.

Interconnected cisterns around the temple meant that the sea could be let in to transform the temple into a water shrine. But, in recent times, a stone wall as been added to protect the shrine from the rising seas and further erosion.

The Shore Temple's main shrine faces the sea with no forecourt or assembly hall leading to it, as was the custom in other contemporary temples.

Yet even with the ceaseless activity of the sea on the one side, and the insidious menace of the drifting sands on the other, its twin towers are still erect and the shrines remain intact, immutable it stands, a silent record of a great but almost forgotten people.

– Percy Brown

The Shore Temple was built by Rajasimha who ascended the throne in AD 674. Unlike the older *rathas* which were hewn out of single rocks, the Shore Temple was the first Pallava structure to be *built* of stone. The greatest improvement in design is in the *shikhara* or spire which has moved away from the rounded *vihara* design to a soaring, tiered style.

This seashore shrine also shows a creative leap in temple architecture of the South. Elements like the *vimana* or spire, the *gopuram* or gateway, and animal figures that were to become trademarks of Dravidian architects can all be seen here. And it is largely the use of dressed stone which gave the architects greater creative freedom.

Arjuna's Penance

This is an immense bas relief, ornately carved on the open face of two adjacent granite rocks. Also called the 'Descent of the Ganga' and 'Bhagiratha's Penance', the carving teems with human figures, animals, deities and ordinary people watching the descent of the holy river from the Himalayas.

The elaborate carvings covering the rock-face have a vibrancy even today.

A natural cleft between the two stones has been creatively used to simulate the cascading Ganga. Among the profusion of figures is an emaciated ascetic (close to the cleft towards the top of the left-hand rock) in the posture of penance. It has been variously identified as Bhagirath beseeching the Ganga to come down to earth and as Arjuna praying to Shiva.

The eastern face of the main hill is covered with carvings depicting the holy river Ganga's descent from Heaven. A water channel has been directed down the crack between two rocks to represent the gushing river. Others have interpreted the scene as Arjuna's Penance.

Fables from the *Panchtantra* and even scenes from daily life are woven into the main carving.

The pillared *mandapas* consisted of a shallow hall leading to an inner shrine.

Mandapas

The main hill at Mamallapuram is dotted with pillared halls carved into the rock face. These *mandapas,* with their graceful columns and intricate figure sculptures bear witness to the artistry of the Pallavan rock-cutter. The ten pavilions at Mamallapuram, of which two are unfinished, were designed as shrines, with a *sanctum* and an outer hall. The shallow porticoes are adorned with exquisite sculptures of gods, goddesses and mythological figures.

The Ganesha *mandapa* is an active shrine even today, with the idol of the elephant-god being revered by the faithful, fourteen centuries after it was first consecrated.

Beyond the circular rock called Krishna's Butterball is the Varaha *mandapa* dedicated to the two *avatars* of Vishnu as Varaha the boar and Vamana the dwarf. The pillars of this pavilion are perhaps the earliest to display a motif that became the signature of southern architecture – the lion pilaster, where a heraldic lion supports an ornamental pillar.

The lion pilasters which became a trademark of Dravidian architecture are first seen in the *mandapas* of Mamallapuram.

The old lighthouse, just above the Mahishasuramardini *mandapa*

The Mahishasuramardini *mandapa* has the goddess Durga in bas relief, slaying a buffalo-headed demon, and the Vishnu Sayana *mandapa* shows Lord Vishnu lying under the protective hood of the seven-headed serpent Adishesha.

Of the other *mandapas*, the Panch Pandava *mandapa*, that is unfinished, has a more elaborate

Inside the Mahishasuramardini *mandapa*. A remarkable example of the fine quality of figure sculpture that adorns the Mamallapuram *mandapas*.

facade. Its pillars are adorned with rearing lions springing from the capital, and the shrine is the only one surrounded by a passage which allows circumbulation.

A precariously-perched rock lovingly referred to as Krishna's Butterball

FESTIVALS

- **Dance Festival** – January
- **Masi Magham** – March
- **Brahmotsava** – April / May
- **Palanquin Ceremony** at the Salasayana Perumal Temple October / November

Rathas

The eight *rathas* are monolithic temples fashioned as chariots. They remain an architectural mystery, for each is apparently a faithful reproduction of a structure built of wood. In fact, even the grain of the timber beams and rafters has been simulated in stone.

The *rathas* are not large, rising to a maximum height of 6 metres. The smallest is the Draupadi *ratha*, which is fashioned as a thatched hut

Of the eight *rathas*, five have been named for the Pandava brothers, the heroes of the epic *Mahabharata*, and their shared wife, Draupadi. The largest is the Dharmaraja *ratha* and it sets the tone for the others. Modelled on a Buddhist *vihara* or monastery, it sports a square hall topped by a vaulting roof. The Bhima, Arjuna and Nakula-Sahdeva *rathas* are lesser copies of the *Dharmaraja ratha.*

The Draupadi *ratha* is the smallest and the quaintest. It is a simple structure, fashioned as a thatched hut borne on the backs of elephants and lions. It was probably the facsimile of a portable village shrine.

The Dharmaraja *ratha*, is dedicated to Yudhishtira, the eldest of the five Pandavas, and best displays the Buddhist influence on early Pallava architecture.

The fact that many of the temples and sculptures of Mamallapuram are unfinished, points to the sudden withdrawal of patronage from rock-cut temples when King Rajasimhavarman came to power.

Tiger Cave: Early Pallavan architects carved their monuments out of whole rocks.

GETTING THERE

By Air:
Chennai (58 kms) is the nearest airport

By Rail:
The nearest railhead is Chengalpet (29 kms) which is linked to Chennai by direct trains.

By Road:
Good roads link to Chennai, Pondicherry and Bangalore. There are daily state tourism buses from Chennai.

Taxis for one day-excursion of Chennai-Mamallapuram-Kanchipuram are also available.

Best time to visit:
November to February

KONARAK

Chariot for the Sun God

The great temple at Konarak was conceived as a colossal chariot of the sun god, Surya, with twelve pairs of exquisitely carved wheels, drawn by seven galloping horses as if emerging from the turbulent waves of the Bay of Bengal.

Today the sea has receded and the temple stands in ruins among the sand dunes, but the Sun Temple is still a magnificent work of art. For centuries, sailors used its looming silhouette as a landmark on the Orissa coast and early European mariners called it the Black Pagoda, while the white-washed Jagannath Temple at Puri was called the White Pagoda. Konarak is today a small village in Puri district of Orissa, connected by road to both Bhubaneswar (65 kms) and Puri (35 kms).

Sun Temple

An exquisitely carved medallion from the spoke of a chariot wheel

According to ancient Hindu texts, Samba, the son of Lord Krishna and his wife Jambavati built the temple. The handsome Samba was cursed by his father for an act of impropriety and got leprosy. After twelve years of severe penance to Surya he was cured. In gratitude he decided to build a temple in honour of Surya. According to *Bhavishya Purana*, Samba brought in the Magis, sun worshippers from Sakadvipa, as local Brahmin priests refused to worship the image. And alien features like boots on the Surya images are due to the influence of these immigrants.

Historically, King Narasimha I of the Ganga dynasty (1238-64) built the temple, locally called Surya Deul. Twelve hundred men worked to complete it in 16 years. As a copperplate inscription of his son, Narasimha II, states with pride, 'King Narasimha built a *mahakutira* (great cottage) at Trikona, a place of great renown, a temple for the sun to live in with the other gods'.

The reason for building this temple is lost in the mists of time. Konarak had been a centre of sun worship and the Surya Deul may have been built at the site of an earlier temple. Some scholars surmise that the temple was erected as a memorial by the ambitious monarch after a victorious military campaign against the Muslims.

In the sixteenth century, Emperor Akbar's biographer, Abul Fazl mentioned the temple in the *Ain-i-Akbari*.

In early 17th century when the Mughals ruled the *suba* of Orissa, the image of Surya was removed to a shrine within the precincts of the Jagannath Temple in Puri. A century later, the Marathas removed the *Aruna Stambha* pillar from the Sun Temple and planted it at its present site in front of Jagannath Temple.

One of the three images of the sun god Surya placed in the niches of the main temple. The use of grey-green chlorite makes for a striking contrast against the surrounding yellow stone.

Forsaken by the presiding deity, the Sun Temple crumbled through neglect and decay. The lofty tower over the *sanctum* collapsed, and by the mid-19th century, when archaeologist James Fergusson visited the site, most of the plinth and the exquisite wheels and horses were engulfed by rising sand from the sea. But as art historian Debala Mitra says, the cruel forces of nature were not alone in bespoiling the beauty of this great monument; it also suffered at the greedy hands of man. The king of Khurdah, for example, removed many of the sculptures to decorate his own fort.

Gigantic lions on elephants flank the entrance to the *bhoga mandapa*, also called the *natya mandir*

Extensive steps were taken for the conservation of this temple by the British government from the beginning of the 20th century. The removal of sand and debris revealed the grandeur of the temple complex for the first time in centuries. The initial task of conservation essential for rendering the monument stable was completed by 1910. At the same time, largescale plantation of trees was undertaken between the temple and the sea to check the advance of drifting sand.

FESTIVALS

- **Konarak Dance Festival:** December
- **Magha Saptami:** January

A panel depicting an army going into battle

GETTING THERE

By Air:
Bhubaneswar (65 kms) is the nearest airport and is connected to all metro cities.

By Rail:
Bhubaneswar (65 kms) and Puri (35 kms) are the nearest railheads.

By Road:
Motorable roads from Bhubaneswar (65 kms) and Puri (35 kms). Buses and taxis available.

Best time to visit:
November to March.

The Sun Temple is the finest example of the Orissa style of temple architecture that includes such fine masterpieces as the Lingaraja Temple in Bhubaneshwar and the Jagannath Temple in Puri.

The seven horses of the Sun Temple symbolise the days of the week and the twelve wheels, the months in a year. The resemblance to a chariot ends with the wheels and the horses, the rest of the temple follows the traditional plan for Orissa temples, consisting of the *rekha deul* or *sanctum*, originally topped with a tower or *shikhara*, that ended in a rounded pyramidal curve.

This is connected to the assembly hall, the *jagamohana*, where the devotees gathered. At a slight distance from the *jagamohana* stands the pillared hall of the *bhoga mandapa* where offerings were made to the gods.

It is the exquisite carvings on the outer walls of the structures at Konarak and the free-standing sculptures that give the temple its

The overwhelming facade of the *bhoga mandapa*

unique character. The friezes cover the platform and walls in sharp contrast to the interiors that are spartan in their plainness.

Walking around the temple you see a dazzling pageantry in stone of musicians and dancers, animals, birds, mythical beasts, kings, queens, nymphs and deities. All the nine *rasas* are depicted here, including panels of erotic sculptures of the sensual *shringara rasa*. Even today these carvings create a vibrant portrait of life in all its glory.

Main Temple

The main temple, the Surya deul, consists of two structures. The *rekha deul* or the *sanctum* where the image of the deity once stood, and the assembly hall or *jagamohana*. It is this structure that is designed as a chariot of the sun god.

Twelve pairs of colossal wheels are carved on the sides of the platform. Each has 16 spokes radiating from the axle, with ornately carved medallions depicting various deities, while the seven horses gallop together beside a broad flight of steps.

Little remains of the *sanctum* except the platform but it does give an idea of the original structure, which was a square chamber with a *shikhara* that rose to over 60 metres. Three larger-than-life statues of Surya, called the *parasa devatas*, were placed in niches of the temple wall. These statues were so placed that they caught the sun's rays at sunrise, noon and sunset.

The ***jagamohana*** or assembly hall remains the best preserved building in the complex. A cubed structure with a tiered pyramidal roof, it has recessed walls creating a large surface area for the opulent carvings. Beautifully proportioned doorways led inside but the interior has been blocked to arrest the subsidence of the walls.

In front of the *jagamohana* but separated by a flight of steps is the ***bhoga mandapa*** where offerings were made to the gods. Some call it the *natya mandir* or dance hall because of the panels of dancers and musicians on the walls. The *Aruna Stambha*, a free-standing pillar in chlorite with the figure of Aruna on its crown originally stood between the *jagamohana* and the *bhoga mandapa*.

MUSEUM

The Archaeological Survey of India runs a museum at the site.

Timing:
9 am to 5 pm.
Closed Thursdays.
Entry free.

The pillared hall no longer has its roof but delightful friezes of dancers and musicians carved on the pillars and walls still survive, giving the *mandapa* an air of permanent celebration.

There are ruins of other structures within the enclosure. A broken door arch has finely carved icons of the *navagraha* or the nine planets. To the southwest is a sanctuary believed to be a temple to Mayadevi, one of the wives of Surya. Also there is a Vaishnava temple with a sanctuary and a porch that was discovered in 1956 and a building probably used as a kitchen.

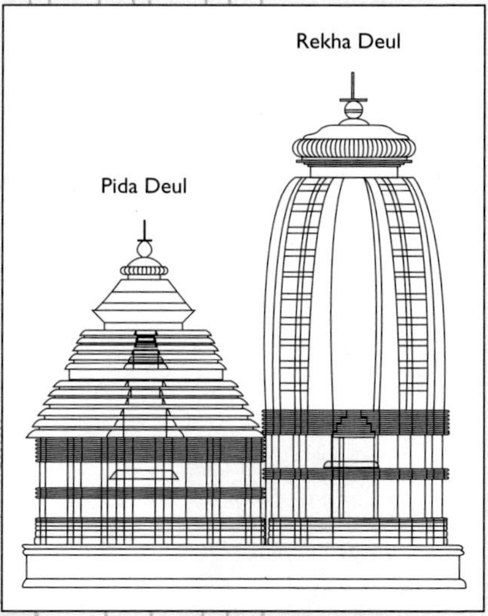

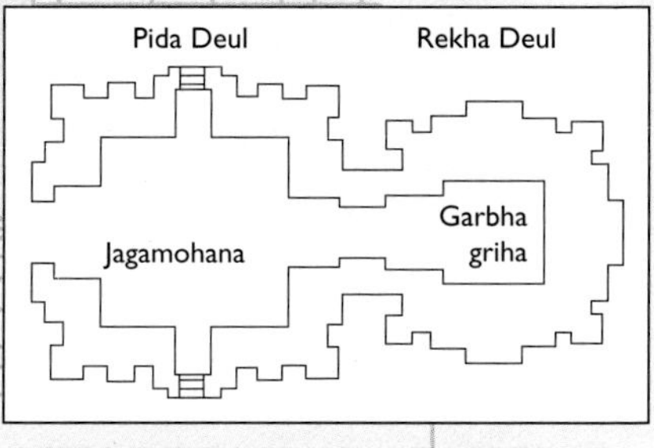

ADAPTED FROM PERCY BROWN, INDIAN ART & ARCHITECTURE

The high quality of the free-standing sculptures and the carvings on the outer walls give Konarak its unique character. Every carving was designed to blend in with the architectural plan of the Surya Deul, creating a temple that is both a brilliant architectural design and a composite showcase of magnificent sculpture.

Among the statues are huge war horses straining at their reins, rampant elephants and lions that show great vitality. In contrast, are the subtle charms of nymphs, dancers, the erotic *mithuna* couples in various moods of lovemaking and the sensual *alasa kanyas* or indolent damsels. Royalty can be seen in processions, parades and hunts.

A carnival of dancers and musicians adorns the platform of the *bhoga mandapa*

Right:
Lingaraja Temple in Bhubaneshwar

The consummate workmanship has effectively captured the fluid grace of the war-horses, which seem to almost pulsate with life

Excursions

Bhubaneswar (65 kms): The capital of the state of Orissa was once the ancient capital of the Kalinga empire. Bhubaneswar has some of the finest temples of the Orissa style. Among those worth visiting is the magnificent Lingaraja Temple. Built in AD 1000 with a 54 metre -high tower that soars over the city. Also visit the Rajarani, Muktesvara, and Brahmesvara temples.

Puri (35 kms): Puri is famous for the Jagannath Temple and its legendary *Rath Yatra* or Car Festival. It has one of the best beaches in eastern India, a broad expanse of sand and turbulent waves.

Friezes of dancers and musicians bring alive the rhythms of life

DARJEELING HIMALAYAN RAILWAY

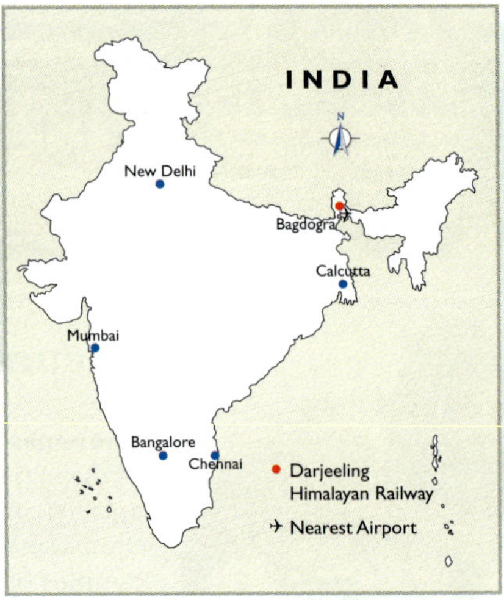

The Darjeeling Himalayan Railway (DHR) is a piece of inspirational railway engineering. A tiny locomotive engine heaves its way up a near-vertical mountain, hauling daily its trainload men and materials up a climb of over 2,000 metres.

Rated amongst the world's most magical railways, the Darjeeling line displays engineering ingenuity in its layout, sterling character in its running and remarkable resilience in its ability to keep steaming into the new millennium. The Guinness Railway Book describes the DHR's ascent, looping and curving its way up the mountain, as 'one of the world's most spectacular' rail journeys.

This tiny locomotive performs the most heroic of tasks, tugging its train up over2,000 metres

The narrow gauge of the track (2 feet) allows the train to progress by adhesion on a tight alignment. Where the hill is too demanding, this Tom Thumb of trains goes at it with a rush and the clever use of reversing stations allows it to gain altitude by zig-zagging.

And then there is the invigorating scenery around Darjeeling. The sensational view of Kanchenjunga, the third highest peak in the world, comes as the finest climax to any journey. The 2,112 metres (6,927 feet) gain in height from New Jalpaiguri – a railway station servicing Siliguri – to Darjeeling, a distance of 88 kms, might be slow but it is never tedious. The dramatic scenery and the audacity of the smoke-spewing locomotive turn this outing into an adventure.

The tortuous haul up the mountain is thirsty work and the little steam engine halts often for water

Darjeeling means Abode of the Thunderbolt and in Tibetan Buddhist lore dragons are said to lurk under its mountains. When the DHR first started, the superstitious were convinced that the railway engineers burrowing into the hill had awakened the dragons. Today, the old engines continue to puff mightily, pulling their blue bogeys up to Darjeeling, now more famed for its high-quality tea than its thunderbolts.

After the British annexed Darjeeling from Sikkim in 1849, they planned to turn it into a sanatorium town and so built a road – later called the Hill Cart Road – for bullock-carts hauling materials up to the new township. Later, tea was smuggled from China and labour from neighbouring Nepal was drafted to lay the extensive tea gardens that, today, make Darjeeling tea one of the world's choicest brews.

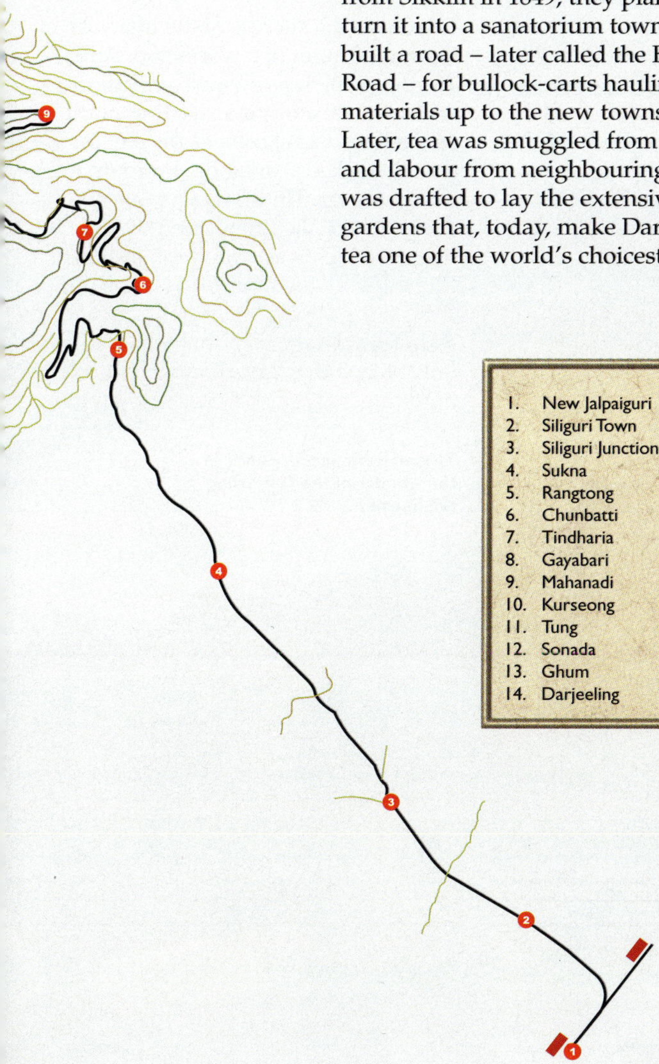

1.	New Jalpaiguri	146 m
2.	Siliguri Town	153 m
3.	Siliguri Junction	156 m
4.	Sukna	163 m
5.	Rangtong	428 m
6.	Chunbatti	673 m
7.	Tindharia	860 m
8.	Gayabari	1,072 m
9.	Mahanadi	1,251 m
10.	Kurseong	1,484 m
11.	Tung	1,725 m
12.	Sonada	1,998 m
13.	Ghum	2,258 m
14.	Darjeeling	2,077 m

In 1879, an agent of the Eastern Bengal Railway, Franklin Prestage, formed a private company to build a tramway that would shadow the Hill Cart Road up the mountain. By 1881, the line to Darjeeling was ready for traffic and the Darjeeling Steam Tramway Company became the Darjeeling Himalayan Railway.
The gauge adopted was 2 feet, the narrowest employed for working purposes and Darjeeling remains the longest hill line in India using this width of track.

Crucial to the success of the line was the establishing of a workshop. And Tindharia, 32 kms away from Siliguri which was the original starting point of the line, was chosen as the site for a well-stocked workshop. From its inception, the Tindharia workshop followed the Victorian creed of self-help to which was added the Indian Railways' virtue of improvisation.

To overcome a terrain that was not only steep but prone to monsoon buffeting – and also to keep down the

The majestic scenery adds to the wonder of the Darjeeling rail journey

cost of construction – Prestage avoided tunnels and bridges and instead used the manoeuvrability of the small engine to go around short radius loops and zig-zag reversing stations to gain height.

The latter, says local lore, was born of a dream. The foreign engineer was frustrated by his inability to push the line forward because of the friable hillside. One night, he dreamt that the god of the mountain said '*Phirangi* (foreigner) go back'. The engineer assumed this indicated defeat but his wife suggested he look at the idea of going back more creatively. Thus was born the Z-reversing station, the gaining of height by switching the train back and forth.

Prestage's calculations worked out advantageously for his private company. The capital was fully subscribed in India to make this railway a source of *swadeshi* or indigenous pride. The cost worked out to Rs 60,000 per mile and incredibly the outlay on rolling stock was only Rs 10,000.

The line was built by Gillander Arbuthnot & Co, and the combination of spiral loops and the clever use of switching to clear the steeper sections is a piece of inspirational engineering. The 88 kms-stretch from the station at New Jalpaiguri to Darjeeling remains a work of railway genius that allows the line to be run on adhesion on an average gradient of 1 in 30.

Before beginning the journey, peep into the tiny engine. Inside, there is barely room for the driver at the regulator and his fireman shovelling coal from a bunker above the water tanks. Steering the tiny locomotive is never easy. The mountain mists make driving the train in reverse – an integral portion of the journey – a nightmare. In fine weather, the driver has to constantly watch out for traffic for the line crosses the Hill Cart Road an incredible 177 times – all at unmanned crossings. And driving in the winters, the engine's headlight suddenly looms like a monster in your path. Little wonder the road traffic scurries to give way to the spooky engine.

Agony Point: The little train goes precariously close to the cliff-edge here

For the first 11 kms to Sukna, the train steams through gentle foothills. At Sukna the little engine already requires water and this raging thirst will be a feature of the ascent to Ghum, the highest point. Between Sukna and Ghum – a distance of nearly 65 kms – the line rises over 2,000 metres or close to 7,000 ft.

Mountain mists are an ever-present hazard for the engine driver

The locomotive smokes hard between Rangtong and Tindharia, as the gradient increases to 1 in 29. The first of the five reversing stations is placed near Rangtong where the train follows a Z shape. It runs forward to a dead-end, backs up the middle stroke of the Z to another dead-end and then accelerates to crest the third portion of rising line.

The section between Tindharia and Gayabari is fairly severe, with loop No. 3 and reversing stations Nos. 4 and 5 in the vicinity. This section also includes 'Agony Point' where the engine seems to overhang the edge as it negotiates a fierce curve of 18 metres radius, the tightest on the line.

Kurseong, the main town on the DHR has come up around the railway line and the trains rattle by so close to the small houses that you can put your hand out and pluck geraniums from the window boxes. The station is plumb in the centre of town and reveals how much of a people's railway the DHR has become. Children run trolleys down the line and their mothers spread their washing to dry between the sleepers. The people of Kurseong have always treated the train with proprietary casualness. They jump on for conversations, wait for the engine to wheeze round the loop, and then climb out again.

After the south-west swing to reach Kurseong, the gradient eases somewhat and Ghum the highest point (some 6 kms short of Darjeeling) is achieved without too much strain. Ghum is often quoted as the highest station in the world but this is only true in the narrow-gauge category. The actual winner is Ticlia Junction in Peru on the standard gauge. The Peru line was built at the same time as the DHR and also uses zig-zags to gain height.

After Ghum, the line drops dramatically at Batasia, in full view of the snow range in the most expansive of the journey's loops. Here the track coils twice around itself to lose height and coast in to Darjeeling some 200 metres lower.

There is no railway scene in the world so nostalgic of the golden age of steam as at Darjeeling terminus. The station building may have been modernised – and rather inelegantly at that – but the loco shed retains its ambience of old. Some of the engines sport nameplates and at least one has seen service for over a hundred years. This is a marvellous tribute to the skill and inventiveness of generations of Tindharia workshop hands.

One of the very first engines to work the line – affectionately called Tiny – is plinthed outside Siliguri station, and a DHR loco sits outside the entrance to Rail Bhawan, the headquarters of the Indian Railways, in New Delhi.

Rungtong watering point

National Rail Museum in New Delhi has an original 1889 engine (Number 777) built in Glasgow. It also has a four-wheeled, third-class wooden passenger coach built in 1902 at Tindharia at a cost of less than Rs 2,000 and which continued in service for 66 years.

Ghum is the highest narrow-gauge railway station in the world

Timings and Entrance

These are the official timings, but the actual running of trains, as well as the time taken, always varies with the weather.

NJ*	Darjeeling
7.30 am	3.15 pm
9 am	5.15 pm

Darjeeling	NJ*
8.25 am	4.20 pm
9.10 am	5.30 pm

Fare:
First Class: Rs 133
Second Class: Rs 25

Kurseong	Darjeeling
(School train)	
6.40 am	9.45 am

Darjeeling	Kurseong
2.30 pm	5.45 pm

Fare:
First Class: Rs 104
Second Class: Rs 17

Ghum Special
Darjeeling Ghum
11 am
Ghum Darjeeling
1 pm

Fare: Rs 200

*NJ: New Jalpaiguri

There is something both heroic and heart-warming about this line. The DHR has a faithful following dedicated to keep it steaming. A locomotives exchange programme is under way with United Kingdom. Luckily, the Darjeeling locomotives are small enough to fit inside a Jumbo jet otherwise the loco exchange could have become a logistical problem!

The DHR achieved its peak operational capacity in 1947, just before the line was taken over by the government. It had 45 locomotives and getting on to 1,450 passenger coaches. But the quaint gauge and the remoteness of the line caused the fleet to dwindle. And as road traffic became faster and more economical, it also began running up losses.

Today, the road transport lobby is averse to the preservation of the DHR and prefers to see the Hill Cart Road widened. Also the 177 crossings across the Hill Cart Road do pose a threat to traffic. The Indian Railways runs it as a 'social cost', which means it bears losses in order to maintain a public service. The grim reality is that for every rupee earned by the DHR the government spends a hundred rupees running it.

To the world at large the line is remembered chiefly for the profile of its sturdy little locomotives taking on the might of the world's highest mountain range. Close up the toy train seems more like a bumper car seconded from a fair ground. Considering they only weigh fifteen and a half tons, the little locomotives have performed manfully and faithfully.

Left:
Chugging through Jorbunglow's narrow streets. The DHR has become a part of the local landscape and life

In 1999 the Darjeeling Himalayan Railway was declared a World Heritage Site by the International Council for Monuments and Sites of the UNESCO. The DHR is 'an outstanding example of the influence of an innovative transportation system on the social, cultural and economic development of a multi-cultural region'.

The decision to include the DHR was capped with a summing up of its significance in railway history: 'The Darjeeling Himalayan Railway is the first and still the most outstanding example of a hill passenger railway'.

PRACTICAL INFORMATION

When to come to India

The best time to come to India is between October and March, when the Indian summer has abated.

However, India is a vast country, stretching across varied climactic zones. The plains of North and Central India, for instance, experience extremes of climate, while the South is more equatorial. The area around Chennai, for example, is hot any time you visit it, and the difference between December and June is merely the difference between hot and hotter.

By and large, however, the winter months remain the most pleasant time to come to India. In the northern plains, the day temperature during December-January can go up to 18°C (64°F) and down to 4°C (39°F) at night. In the South, temperatures hover around 32°C (89°F) even in winter.

After the scorching summer come the monsoon rains. But the arrival of the rains also varies from region to region. The South gets the monsoon in October-November, the western region from early June to the end of August, the East from early June to September and the plains of the North from early July to mid-September.

What to wear

India does not have a fixed dress code, but it would be sensible to wear comfortable clothes which do not attract unnecessary attention. Loose cotton clothes are useful everywhere during the summer months, as is a scarf or hat to protect your head from the blazing sun.

Winter in the North can be very cold so take along a windcheater or jacket to wear over a cardigan or sweater. The South has nothing approaching a winter, and a light wrapper for the evening should suffice. Darjeeling in the hills of the eastern Himalayas can be exceptionally cold, so go prepared.

Where to stay

In major Indian cities, you will find a wide range of accommodation – from deluxe five-star hotels that are as good as the best in the world, through middle-range hotels and guest-houses that are well-appointed, to the lower-end tourist lodges.

Delhi, Mumbai, Chennai, Bangalore, Goa and Agra all have a number of high-end luxury hotels. These offer a wide range of personal and business facilities and bookings can be made by phone or fax.

But, do remember that over and above the room rent in the deluxe and five-star categories, the government levies an additional luxury tax, as well as taxes on expenditure and food and beverages. All air-conditioned hotels will also have a hotel entertainment tax.

The budget hotels and low-end tourist lodges in most towns are located around the railway stations. These are usually functional but well-serviced. The checking-out hour is usually noon for the larger hotels, although some smaller ones compute the tariff according to every 24 hours of stay.

Apart from hotels, other options include guest houses, retiring rooms at airports and railway stations (you need a valid ticket to use either), and charitable dormitories in *dharamshalas* and *gurudwaras* run by Hindu and Sikh trusts respectively. Youth hostels and camping sites are options that students and backpackers might also consider.

Before coming to India

There are a few things you need to take care of before travelling to India.

Visa

There are three kinds of visas for tourists.

1. The 15-day single/double-entry transit visa. This visa is valid for 30 days from the date of its issue.
2. The 3-month multiple-entry visa. This visa is valid for 90 days from the date of first entry into India, which must be within 30 days from the date of its issue.
3. The 6-month multiple-entry visa. This visa is valid for 180 days from the date of its issue, not from the date of entry into India.

Visa Extension

It is virtually impossible to get the 15-day or 3-month visa extended. Only the 6-month tourist visa can be extended. It can be quite a bother to extend it beyond a 15-day period. Avoid it unless there is an emergency.

A 15-day extension on the 6-month visa is issued by the **Foreigner's Regional Registration Office (FRRO) at any of the four metros: Delhi, Calcutta, Chennai, Mumbai**. The FRRO office is open on weekdays, 9.30 am to 1.30 pm and 2 pm to 4 pm. A 15-day extension is given only if confirmed air tickets are not available. No fee is charged.

- **New Delhi**: FRRO
  Hans Bhawan,
  1st Floor, Bahadur Shah Zafar Marg
  Ph 3319781
- **Calcutta**: FRRO
  237 A J C Bose Road
  Ph 2473300
- **Chennai**: FRRO
  Shastri Bhawan,
  Haddows Road, Nungambakkam
  Ph 8275424
- **Mumbai**: FRRO
  Dr D N Road,
  (near Police Commissioners Office)
  Ph 2621169

Travel Insurance

Take a travel insurance policy, covering theft and loss, before coming to India. Also get a medical insurance. There are several kinds of insurance policies. Make the right choice after consulting a reliable travel agent in your country.

Driving Licence

A valid International Driving Licence is necessary if you wish to drive a car or a motorcycle in India and it is advisable to get one before coming. If you do not have an International Driving Licence and still wish to drive in India, you can get a Temporary Driving Licence, provided you are carrying a valid driving licence of your country. You may still be required to give a test to check your knowledge of road signs.

Health

Your health during your travel in India depends on three things: Precautions taken before arrival, day-to-day health care, and efficiency in tackling emergencies.

No particular vaccination is required for coming to India. However, visitors from designated countries in Africa, South America and Papua New Guinea, even if they are on transit, are required to bring valid Yellow Fever vaccination certificates. In the absence of this certificate they will be quarantined for six days.

Precautionary medication is the best bet against common ailments like diarrhoea, dysentry and malaria. Malaria is a problem in India especially during the rainy season. So, if you are coming at that time of the year, do consult your doctor for precautionary anti-malarial medication. While in India, use a mosquito repellent.

For travel health, use your common sense. Take care of what you eat or drink. This is the most important health rule. Water is suspect, therefore, it is best to carry your own mineral water. Bottled mineral water and aerated drinks are easily avaliable and are a good substitute for water. Hot tea and coffee are also good alternatives.

If you are not already vaccinated against Hepatitis B, get it done before travelling.

Those not accustomed to Indian conditions are usually vulnerable to stomach problems. It is advisable to seek qualified medical advice before travelling and carry your own first-aid kit. Aspirins, antiseptic cream, oral rehydration salts and anti-histamines are a must. Please carry medical prescriptions for antibiotics which may be required. These are not available over the counter.

Diarrhoea is the most common stomach ailment. Take a three or five-day course of anti-diarrhoea tablets duly prescribed by a doctor.

Diarrhoea leads to dehydration. So, along with medication, drink a lot of water with salt and sugar. There are some restrictions on your diet, too. Alcohol, milk, meat, fried and spicy foods should be avoided. If the bout of upset stomach persists, get a stool test done because it might be amoebic dysentery.

The tropical sun is extremely strong during the summer months, so guard against sun stroke and dehydration. Wear a hat and dark glasses when you go out. Drink lots of non-alcoholic liquids, water and fruit juice. Allow sweat to evaporate, wear loose cotton clothes. Use calamine or sunscreen lotion and talcum powder as a precaution against prickly heat rash.

Emergencies

All big cities have both government and privately-run hospitals and nursing homes. Medical assistance in government hospitals is slow due to large patient turnout. Service at privately-run hospitals and nursing homes is usually better.

Food

You will be overwhelmed by the variety of Indian food and if you are adventurous about food, you will have a wonderful time trying out the tastes of India. The major metros offer good food from all over the world, the traveller will not be homesick for his own kind of food. A foreigner may also find it worth sampling Indian food. The restaurants are varied, not only in their ambience, but also in their rates.

Most big hotels have multi-cuisine restaurants, often with bars. Some of the better known restaurants are in five-star hotels. Though not easy on the pocket, they are probably the safest in terms of hygiene.

Be careful of what you eat and drink, especially from the innumerable streetside vendors (*dhabas*). Fresh fruits are always a safe bet.

Things you can bring to India

Visitors can bring in articles for personal use, including cameras with 5 rolls of film, a reasonable quantity of jewellery, a pair of binoculars, a portable musical instrument, a portable radio, a tape recorder, a portable typewriter, a laptop computer and professional equipment. On arrival, you will have to give an undertaking on a Tourist Baggage Re-Export (TBRE) form, available with Customs officials at the airport, that you will take these items back when you leave. This form, along with the articles that are entered in it, have to be shown to the Customs officials at the time of leaving India.

Designated 'high-value articles' are also allowed in, but on a written undertaking that they will be taken back at the time of departure. Please obtain a Landing Certificate if you are expecting unaccompanied baggage and for mishandled baggage.

You can bring in 200 cigarettes (or 50 cigars or 250 gms of tobacco) and liquor and wine up to 32 oz (1 litre).

You are allowed to bring in any amount of foreign currency in cash or travellers' cheques. However, if you are carrying more than US $ 2500 (or equivalent), you have to declare it on arrival. Fill up the Currency Declaration Form (CDF) which is to be attested by the Customs Officer. Indian currency cannot be brought in nor taken out of the country.

Things you can take back

Export Regulations

A visitor can take back the following goods:

A. Souvenirs (including Indian silk, wool, handicrafts, etc.) without any limit.

B. Gold jewellery and silverware up to a value of Rs 100,000 (and in excess of that only after obtaining a permit from the RBI, the Indian central bank).

C. Other jewellery and precious stones, but if of high value, these should be appraised by the Customs Appraiser at the airport before departure. As a general rule, get an RBI permit for goods of high value. There are also restrictions on export of antiques and art objects which are more than 100 years old. In case of doubt, consult the Director, Antiquities, **Archaeological Survey of India**, Janpath, New Delhi (Ph 3012191). It is advisable to get a certificate of proof.

Export of most wildlife products is either prohibited or strictly regulated. Do not buy articles made of ivory, reptile, tiger or deer skin, tortoise shell or shahtoosh shawls made by killing the Tibetan antelope.

Tax Clearance Certificate

If you stay in India for more than 120 days (4 months), from the date of issue of the visa, regardless of your date of entry into India, you would be required to furnish a tax clearance certificate to leave the country. This is to prove that you did not earn money while in India and that your trip was financed with the money brought in. If you are planning to stay in India for more than four months, be careful with your documents relating to travel finance.

If you are not an Indian passport holder and you are planning to stay in India for more than four months, apply for the certificate at the **Income Tax Department**, Central Revenue Building (ITO), Vikas Marg, New Delhi. (Ph 3316161/3319198).

Foreign Travel Tax

Rs 500 has to be paid at the airport as Foreign Travel Tax when leaving the country. For travel to Pakistan, Nepal, Sri Lanka, Bhutan, Myanmar, the Maldives and Afghanistan, the tax is Rs 150.

There are two channels for customs clearance at International terminals in Indian airports: Green Channel and Red Channel.

Green Channel: This is for unhindered exit from the airport. You can walk through the Green Channel if you are not carrying goods which attract customs duty.

Red Channel: For those who have anything to declare, including money worth more than US $2500.

Transfer from Airport

Taxis: There are pre-paid taxi counters in the arrival area of all major airports. It is a good idea to hire a pre-paid taxi to avoid being overcharged.

Coaches: There are coach services for transfer into the city at most airport terminals.

Auto rickshaws: They carry up to three passengers and are cheaper than cabs. They are available outside some Indian airports, though the fare may have to be negotiated.

Travel within India

Travelling by Air

There are several airlines that fly to domestic destinations. The biggest is Indian Airlines, a state-owned domestic carrier. Other major flyers are Alliance Air, a subsidiary of Indian Airlines, Jet Airways and Sahara India Airlines.

Hand Baggage: In all domestic flights, passengers are allowed one piece of hand baggage. All baggage is subject to security check, whether carried by hand or booked in the hold.

Baggage Allowance: Domestic airlines allow 20 kgs check-in baggage for Economy Class and 30 kgs for Business Class. Excess baggage is charged as per the schedule available at the airline's counter.

The reporting time for all domestic flights is 60 minutes prior to departure.

Indian Airlines offers two special travel packages (if paid for in US dollars):

Discover India Fare: US $500 for 15 days and US $750 for 21 days of unlimited travel with certain routing restrictions.

India Wonderfare: US $300 for 7 days of unlimited travel.

Travelling by Rail

The Indian Railways run a gigantic, modern and organised network which connects the metropolitan cities to most major and minor destinations across the length and breadth of India.

Time Zone

Indian Standard Time (IST) is 5½ hours ahead of Greenwich Mean Time and 10½ hours ahead of US Eastern Standard Time. IST is 4½ hours behind Australian Eastern Standard Time, 3½ hours behind Japanese Standard Time and 1½ hours behind Thai Standard Time.

Despite its vast geographical territory, India has just one time zone, and no daylight saving time in summer.

Trains in India are very crowded and it is necessary to reserve a seat or a berth to travel in any degree of comfort.

Rail reservations start from 60 days before the date of travel. Reservations can be cancelled up to 24 hours before the train leaves, but a nominal cancellation fee has to be paid.

Train tickets must be bought before you enter the train. You will be penalised if you do not have one and intend to buy it on board.

International Travel Bureau on the first floor of New Delhi railway station is open Monday through Saturday, 7.30 am to 5 pm. Tickets here are issued only to foreign nationals and non-resident Indians against payment in US dollars.

Such tickets get a priority on reservation under the Foreign Tourist Quota and are exempted from reservation fees.

Indrail Passes for travel in India by train can be booked in India or abroad. The fare has to be paid in foreign currency. The passes are valid for 1 to 90 days. You can buy Indrail passes at the railway reservation offices in the following cities connected to the World Heritage circuit: New Delhi, Mumbai, Calcutta, Chennai, Agra Cantt, Bangalore, and Vasco da Gama. Certain travel agents in Delhi, Mumbai, Calcutta and Chennai are also authorised to sell these passes.

Indrail Pass Prices in US $

Days	Air-cond.	1stclass	2nd class
7	270	135	80
15	370	185	90
21	396	198	100
30	495	248	125
60	800	400	185
90	1060	530	235

Porters: All stations have a licenced porter facility. They sport a metal armband with a number on it. It is advisable to use the services of the licenced porter or coolie.

If you are arriving by a late night train and happen to be in an Indian railway station for the first time, it is possibly the safest place to stay until morning. There are upper class waiting rooms in all stations, as well as retiring rooms.

Transport from the Station: Taxis and auto rickshaws are available in major railway stations. Buses are also available but they are likely to be crowded.

Travelling by Road

According to a recent study, there are over 15 different modes of road transportation by which people manoeuvre their way around India, ranging from Mercedes Benz cars to the humble bullock cart. The level of noise in the streets of an Indian city may unnerve the first time visitor.

Auto Rickshaw: No visit to India can be complete without a ride on an auto rickshaw a three-wheeled, black-and-yellow, canopied contraption. These little vehicles are allowed to carry up to three passengers at a time. Auto rides are no joy rides, especially over bumpy roads with no discretion shown for speed. They are, however, a cheap way to travel from point to point.

Cycle Rickshaw: Cycle rickshaws are a common sight in most parts of urban and rural India. They are a convenient means of covering short distances. Not only do they precariously balance two or three persons, but often carry merchandise as well.

Money

Indian Currency

The Indian currency is called the Rupee. It is available in denominations of 500, 100, 50, 20, 10, 5, 2, 1. One rupee equals 100 paise. Coins in common use are those of Rs 5, Rs 2 , Re 1 and 50 and 25 paise. The 20, 10 and 5 paise coins have become redundant in big cities, but they still have value in smaller towns and in rural India.

ATM Service

All metros have ATM (automatic teller machine) services run by foreign and Indian banks and are open 24 hours. Instructions are given in English and the cash dispensed is in rupees.

Credit Cards

Credit cards are becoming increasingly popular in urban areas. All major international credit cards are accepted.

Banks

Most international banks have branches in the major cities, so encashing travellers' cheques or changing foreign currency is fairly simple.

Indian state-run banks are open from 10 am to 2 pm Monday to Friday and from 10 am to 12 pm on Saturdays. They are closed on Sundays and national holidays. However, privately-run Indian banks and international banks have more flexible hours.

While all major cities have a large number of banks, small towns are pretty inadequate in their banking services.
So, you are best advised to complete all financial transactions in the larger cities.

Local Conveyance

Taxis and auto-rickshaws are available in all cities, although only those in the metros are metred. In other places, it is best to fix the rate beforehand. And to bargain.

The vehicles which do have metres will also carry a rate-chart that will allow you to calculate the actual amount to be paid.

The metros also have several kinds of taxis on their roads: yellow-topped taxis for city travel, and white tourist cars, both air-conditioned and non air-conditioned.

There are counters for pre-paid taxis in airports as well as outside major railway stations. It is a good idea to hire a pre-paid taxi to avoid being over-charged.

You can hire a private taxi for local and outstation tours at most hotels and airports. Within city limits, the rates are approximately Rs 450 for eight hours or 80 kms in a non air-conditioned Ambassador car or Maruti van, and Rs 750 for an air-conditioned car. Outstation travel will cost you Rs 5.50 per km, provided you are travelling a minimum of 100 kms. Overnight charges are Rs 150 per night.

International car rental companies, as well as Indian private companies also run car-rental services. Most metros also have a dial-a-cab service.

It is probably not a good idea to take a bus for local travel – especially if you have luggage.

International Airlines Offices

Airlines/City	City Office Ph	Airport Ph
Air India		
Delhi	3736446, 3736447	5653132
Bangalore	2277747	6263491
Chennai	8554488	2340551
Mumbai	2013031	8366767
Air France		
Delhi	3738004, 3312853	5652294
Bangalore	5587258, 5589214	NA
Chennai	8554894, 8554899	NA
Mumbai	8328070, 8323072	2025021
Alitalia		
Delhi	3311019, 3354666	5652348
Bangalore	5591936, 5592156	NA
Chennai	4349432, 4349822	2347348
Mumbai	2045026, 2045027	8342622 8216981
British Airways		
Delhi	3329906, 3323099	5652908
Bangalore	2997324, 2271205	NA
Chennai	8554680, 8554756	2332351
Mumbai	2820888	8329061 8329063
Gulf Air		
Delhi	3324293, 3327814	5652065
Bangalore	5580857, 5584702	NA
Chennai	8554417	8554417
Mumbai	2021626	8327588
Japan Airlines		
Delhi	3327104, 3327108	5653358
Bangalore	2245560	NA
Chennai	8592333, 8592335	NA
Mumbai	2833136, 2833215	NA
KLM		
Delhi	3357747, 3324489	5652420
Bangalore	2265562, 2268703	NA
Chennai	8524427, 8524437	NA
Mumbai	2833338	8380492

Airlines/City	City Office Ph	Airport Ph
Lufthansa		
Delhi	3323310, 3327268	5652064
Bangalore	5588791, 5587545	NA
Chennai	8525095, 8525197	2340551
Mumbai	2025322, 2833936	8366700
Pakistan International Airlines		
Delhi	3737791, 3737794	5652841
Mumbai	2021455	NA
Royal Nepal Airlines		
Delhi	3321164, 3323437	5696876
Mumbai	2836197, 2836198	NA
SAS		
Delhi	3352299, 3350307	5653708
Bangalore	2219810, 2219820	NA
Chennai	8262315	NA
Mumbai	2027083	NA
Singapore Airlines		
Delhi	3321624, 3350131	5653072
Chennai	8522871	2344680
Mumbai	2023316, 2022747	8356887
Swissair		
Delhi	3722993, 3722994	5652535
Bangalore	8524783	NA
Chennai	8522541, 8424783	NA
Mumbai	2872210, 2872494	8350424
Thai Airways		
Delhi	6239988	5652796
United Airlines		
Delhi	3351265, 3353377	5653910
Calcutta	2801630, 2801731	5118189
Bangalore	2244621, 2244622	NA
Chennai	8226290, 8226291	NA
Mumbai	2047027, 2875944	NA
Virgin Airlines		
Delhi	3368674, 3368675	5655747

Police Assistance Booths

Police assistance booths are located at airports, railway stations and near the major bus stands.

Lost articles: In case of loss or theft, especially of vital documents like passports, an FIR (First Information Report) must be filed at the Police Station closest to the place where the loss occured. In case of loss of documents, the embassy or high commission concerned must be immediately informed.

Communications

Post Offices

The main post offices in large towns provide a wide range of facilities like telegraph, fax and a courier service which operates under the brand name EMS-Speed Post.

If you need to dispatch a letter or document urgently it might be advisable to send it by the government-run Speed Post.

Parcels by mail should not exceed 20 kgs. Books, documents, papers and printed material can be sent by book post which costs less.

All Post Offices are open from 10 am to 5:30 pm Monday to Saturday.

Telephone

ISD (international), **STD** (domestic long distance), and local telephone booths are available all over India.

The rates for international calls are fixed, but calls within the country are charged on the basis of a pulse rate which varies for different cities, and for different times of the day.

E-mail

All metros and most major cities have numerous cyber cafes that allow you to send and receive e-mail for a nominal charge.

STD Codes

Agra	0562
Ajanta	02438
Aurangabad	0240
Badami	08357
Bagdogra	03556
Bangalore	080
Bhopal	0755
Bhubaneshwar	0674
Calcutta	033
Chennai	044
Darjeeling	0354
Delhi	011
Ellora	02437
Fatehpur Sikri	05619
Hampi	08394
Jhansi	0517
Khajuraho	07686
Konarak	06758
Mamallapuram	04113
Mumbai	022
Panjim (Goa)	0832
Sanchi	07592
Siliguri	0353
Thanjavur	04362
Thiruchirapalli	0431

Phrase Book : English-Hindi

In Emergencies

help!
bachao!

stop
ruko

medicines
davai

Please call a doctor/ ambulance
doctor/ambulance ko bulaiye

Where is the nearest hospital?
nazdeek hospital kahan hai?

I'm not feeling well
Meri tabiyat theek nahin hai

Where is... ?
Kahan hai...?

When will... be back?
...vaapas kab ayenge?

Call the police
Police ko bulaiye

Essential words

greetings	***namaste/ namaskar***
yes	***haan***
no	***nahin***
thank you	***dhanyavad/ shukriya***
money	***paisa/ rupaye***
time	***samay***
day	***din***
night	***raat***
morning	***subah***
evening	***shaam***
afternoon	***dopeher***
today	***aaj***
tomorrow	***kal***
yesterday	***kal***
here	***idhar/yahan***
there	***udhar/wahan***
food	***khaana***
water	***paani***
girl	***ladki***
boy	***ladka***
woman	***aurat***
man	***aadmi***
who	***kaun***
why	***kyon***
what	***kya***
where	***kahan***
when	***kab***
how	***kaise***
one/two	***ek/do***
hot	***garam***
cold	***thanda***

Shopping

What is this?	***Yeh kya hai?***
clothes	***kapda***
shoes	***joota***
big	***bara***
small	***chhota***
black	***kala***
white	***safed***
red	***lal***
blue	***neela***
yellow	***peela***
green	***hara***

good	***achha***
bad	***bura***
open	***khula***
close	***band***
left	***baayen***
right	***daayen***
near	***paas***
far	***dur***
up	***oopar***
down	***neeche***
outside	***bahar***
inside	***andar***
fast	***jaldi***
slow	***dheere***
car	***gaadi***
bus	***bus***
road	***sadak***
way	***raasta***
house	***ghar, makaan***
door	***darwaaza***
fan	***pankha***
electricity	***bijlee***
train	***train, rail gaadi***
aeroplane	***hawai jahaz***

Useful Phrases

How are you?
Aap kaise hain?

Very well, thank you
Hum theek hain, dhanyavad

What is your name?
Aap ka naam kya hai?

My name is...
Mera naam...hai

See you
Phir milenge

What is the time?
Kitna baja hai?

Where are you from?
Aap kahan se aaye hain?

Do you speak English?
Kya aap angrezi bolte hain?

Do you have change?
Khule paise milenge?

Do you have...
Aap ke paas...hai?

How much does this cost?
Yeh kitne ka hai ?

Do you take credit cards?
Aap credit card lete hain?

How far is...
Kitna door hai?

Tips or Baksheesh

There is no rule which compels you to tip anyone for any service rendered. Courtesy demands that you tip a waiter in a restaurant or hotel. The general norm is to pay 10% of the billed amount. Taxis, auto rickshaws, public transport staff, government officials or private service providers are not expected to be tipped. It is entirely up to you to tip someone for services rendered.

Sometimes the urge to tip can be misunderstood, as it may be considered an assault on dignity.

TRAVELLERS' NEEDS

WORLD HERITAGE CULTURAL SITES IN INDIA

1. Qutb Minar
2. Humayun's Tomb
3. Agra Fort
4. Taj Mahal
5. Fatehpur Sikri
6. Sanchi
7. Khajuraho
8. Elephanta Cave
9. Ajanta Caves
10. Ellora Caves
11. Old Goa
12. Pattadakal
13. Hampi
14. Brihadisvara
15. Mamallapuram
16. Konarak
17. Darjeeling Himalayan Railway

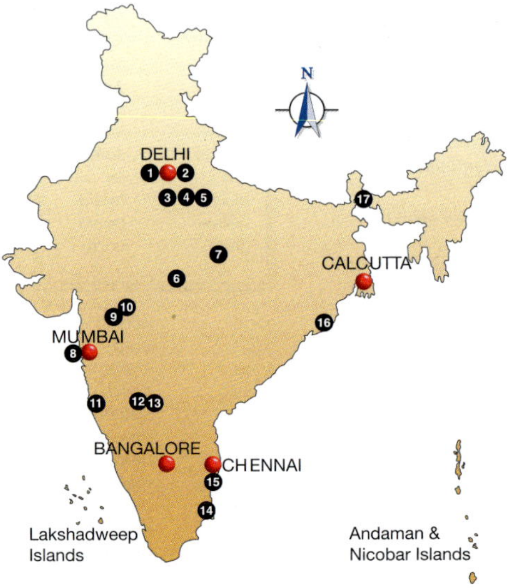

DELHI

STD Code : 011

Humayun's Tomb • Qutb Minar

As the capital of India, Delhi not only has a well-serviced international airport but is also the obvious point from where to make connections for most parts of the country.

Delhi has two World Heritage sites, the Qutb Minar and Humayun's Tomb. The other sites in North India – the Taj Mahal and Agra Fort in Agra, the abandoned city of Fatehpur Sikri near Agra, the Buddhist *stupas* at Sanchi, and the famous temples of Khajuraho – are all within easy reach.

Arriving by Air

Delhi's international airport is 19 kms away from the city centre at Connaught Place and the domestic airport 12 kms away. For the Heritage circuit, Delhi is connected to Agra, Khajuraho and Bhopal – the airport closest to Sanchi – by air. Flight schedules can be checked from the airline offices listed here:

Airport Enquiry Terminal 1 (Domestic)
Ph 5665121

Airport Enquiry Terminal 2 (International)
Ph 5652011, 5652021

Airline Offices

Indian Airlines
Malhotra Bldg, F Block, Connaught Place
Ph 3310517

PTI Bldg, Sansad Marg , Ph 3710369

Safdarjang Airfield, Aurobindo Marg
Ph 4622220 (24-hour office)

Airport Ph 5665121

Alliance Air (a subsidiary of Indian Airlines)

Airport Ph 5665313

Jet Airways
13 Community Centre, Yusuf Sarai
Ph 6853700 (24-hour office)

Airport Ph 5665404, 5665405

Sahara India
Ambadeep Bldg, 14 Kasturba Gandhi Marg
Ph 3326851, 3326853

Airport Ph 5665234, 5665875

Air India
Scindia House, Janpath Road
Ph 3736446, 3736447

Airport Ph 5652041, 5653132

Arriving by Train

Delhi has three railway stations, the New Delhi Railway Station (RS), Hazrat Nizamuddin RS, and Old Delhi RS, and is extremely well connected to all parts of the country. Agra, Jhansi (for Khajuraho) and Bhopal (for Sanchi) are linked to Delhi by many good trains. We recommend the daily Shatabdi Express (train no 2002) leaving New Delhi RS daily at 6 am and servicing all three destinations.

Railway Enquiry
Ph 131, 1330, 1335, 1345

Ticket Reservation

Delhi is a good place to buy onward and return journey tickets. The **International Travel Bureau** on the first floor of New Delhi railway station has a special booking office for foreigners. It is open Monday through Saturday, 7.30 am to 5 pm. Tickets here are issued only to foreign nationals and non-resident Indians against payment in US dollars.

Arriving by Road

Road Distances from Delhi

Agra	204 kms
Ajmer	450 kms
Alwar	160 kms
Bharatpur	183 kms
Bhopal	700 kms
Chandigarh	250 kms
Dehradun	230 kms
Fatehpur Sikri	238 kms
Gwalior	320 kms
Haridwar	220 kms
Jaipur	250 kms
Jhansi	415 kms
Khajuraho	590 kms
Mathura	146 kms
Mussoorie	270 kms
Pushkar	462 kms
Rishikesh	238 kms
Sanchi	750 kms
Varanasi	785 kms
Vidisha	760 kms

Bus

Delhi is connected by bus to all major destinations in north India. The main bus stands are the Inter-State Bus Terminals – better known as the ISBTs – at Kashmere Gate, Sarai Kale Khan and Anand Vihar.

Roadways Enquiry

ISBT Kashmere Gate	2968836
ISBT Sarai Kale Khan	4638092
ISBT Anand Vihar	2152431
Delhi Transport Corpn	2968836
Haryana Roadways	2961262
Himachal Roadways	2966725
Punjab Roadways	2967842
Rajasthan Roadways	2961246
UP Roadways	2968709

GETTING AROUND

Car Rentals

There are several international and local companies that operate car rental services. Most car rentals accept international credit cards. Foreign nationals are required to pay in foreign exchange, unless exempted by the Reserve Bank of India.

Hertz, Europcar and others have rates which are on a 4 hours and 40 kms, or 8 hours and 80 kms basis, with and without chauffeurs. The rates vary according to the choice of car. Valid driving licence, proof of residence and copy of passport (in case of foreigners) are required.

Guided Tours

The stated-owned ITDC as well as several private travel agents conduct tours to Agra, Jaipur, Mathura and Rishikesh, besides other tourist destinations.

Ashok Tours & Travels (ITDC)
305 New Delhi House, Barakhamba Road
Ph 3715917

(Pick-up points: Hotel Kanishka, Hotel Janpath, Hotel Lodhi and Hotel Ashok Yatri Niwas)

Delhi Tourism
Ph 3363607, 3365358

(Pick-up point: Coffee Home on Baba Kharak Singh Marg)

Delhi Transport Corporation (DTC)
Ph 3317445

(Pick-up point: Scindia House in Connaught Place)

Government of India Tourism Office
88 Janpath, Ph 3320005

(Pick-up points: 88 Janpath and Hotel Ashok Yatri Niwas)

Tourist Information Centres

Government of India
88 Janpath, Ph 3320008

Delhi
36 N-Block, Middle Circle
Connaught Place, Ph 3315322

Goa
18 Amrita Shergil Marg, Ph 4629967

Karnataka
Karnataka Bhawan II
Sardar Patel Marg, Ph 4102263

Madhya Pradesh
Kanishka Shopping Complex
19 Ashoka Road, Ph 3341187, 3366528

Orissa
B-4, Emporia Complex
Baba Kharak Singh Marg, Ph 3364580

Sikkim
New Sikkim House, 14 Panchsheel Marg
Chanakyapuri, Ph 6115171

Tamil Nadu
C1, Baba Kharak Singh Marg, Ph 3735427

UP Tourism
Chandralok Building, 36 Janpath
Ph 3322251

West Bengal
A2, Emporia Complex
Baba Kharak Singh Marg, Ph 3732840

Where to shop

Delhi is the best place to pick up a selection of Indian handicrafts. Government-run emporia source them from all over the country and you can be assured of both the price and the authenticity.

Ambawatta Complex, Mehrauli Village

Central Cottage Industries Emporium, Janpath

Dilli Haat, Aurobindo Marg

Hauz Khas Village

Khadi Gramodyog Bhawan, Connaught Place

Palika Bazaar, Connaught Place

Qutab Colonnade, Mehrauli Road

Santushti Complex, Chanakyapuri

State Emporia, Baba Kharak Singh Marg

Other popular markets in Delhi

Ajmal Khan Road, Karol Bagh

Central Market, Lajpat Nagar

Sarojini Nagar Market

Book Shops

Bright Book Bureau
239/31 Gali Kunjash, Dariba Kalan
Chandni Chowk, Ph 3273681

Bahri & Sons
Khan Market, Ph 4694610

Faqir Chand & Sons
Khan Market, Ph 4618810

Prakash Book Depot
M-86, Connaught Place
Ph 3326566, 3326897

Lov Dev & Sons
4 Upper Basement, Surya Kiran Building
19 Kasturba Gandhi Marg
Ph 3718081, 3311844

Midlands
Aurobindo Place Market, Ph 6867121

The Bookworm
29 B-Block, Connaught Place
Ph 3322260

The Bookshop
Khan Market, Ph 4697102

Variety Book Depot
M-3, AVG Bhawan,
Middle Circle, Connaught Place
Ph 3327175, 3344567

Where to stay

Apart from a string of luxury hotels, Delhi has much to offer the budget traveller. Most of these low-priced tourist lodges are located in the Connaught Place/ Paharganj area, as also in the Old City.

Vishwa Yuvak Kendra
Circular Road, Chanakyapuri
Ph 3013631, 3013632

YMCA Tourist Hostel
Jai Singh Road, Connaught Place
Ph 3746031, Fax 3746032

Youth Hostel
5 Nyaya Marg, Chanakyapuri
Ph 6116285

YWCA
Blue Triangle Family Hostel
Ashok Road, Connaught Place
Ph 3735138

YWCA International Guest House
10 Sansad Marg, Connaught Place
Ph 3361561

Basic accommodation is also available for a maximum of three days against a valid train ticket at the following:

Retiring Rooms
New Delhi Railway Station
Ph 3733222

Rail Yatri Niwas
Ajmeri Gate, Ph 3233484

Hotels

Average rack rate in rupees for a standard double room

Ⓐ Above 6000 Ⓑ 4000-6000 Ⓒ 2500-4000 Ⓓ 1500-2500 Ⓔ Below 1500

Ⓐ **Hyatt Regency**
Bhikaji Cama Place
Ph 6791234, Fax 6796833

Ⓐ **Imperial**
Janpath
Ph 3341234, Fax 3342255

Ⓐ **Maurya Sheraton**
Sardar Patel Marg
Ph 6112233, Fax 6113333

Ⓐ **Oberoi**
Dr Zakir Hussain Marg
Ph 4363030, Fax 4360484

Ⓐ **Park Royal**
Nehru Place
Ph 6223344, Fax 6224288

Ⓐ **Radisson**
National Highway 8
Ph 6129191, Fax 6129090

Ⓐ **Taj Palace**
Sardar Patel Marg, Ph 6110202, Fax 6110808

Ⓐ **Taj Mahal**
Mansingh Road
Ph 3026162, Fax 3026070

Ⓑ **Ambassador**
Sujan Singh Park
Ph 4632600, Fax 4638219

Ⓑ **Kanishka**
Ashoka Road
Ph 3344422, Fax 3368242

Ⓑ **The Claridges**
Aurangzeb Road
Ph 3010211, Fax 3010625

Ⓒ **Nirula's**
L-Block, Connaught Place
Ph 3322419, Fax 3324669

Ⓒ **Qutab**
Shaheed Jeet Singh Marg
Ph 6521010, Fax 6968287

Ⓓ **Jukaso Inn Down Town**
L-1 Connaught Circus
Ph 3324451, 3324452, Fax 3324448

Ⓓ **Lodhi**
Lala Lajpat Rai Marg
Ph 4362422, Fax 4362082

Ⓔ **Indraprastha**
Ashoka Road
Ph 3344511, Fax 3368153

AGRA

STD Code : 0562

Agra Fort • Taj Mahal • Fatehpur Sikri

Agra is home to the Taj Mahal, probably the most enduring symbol of India and one of the most sought-after tourist destinations in the world. Being only 204 kms (about 3 hours' drive) from Delhi, Agra is very popular with both foreign and domestic tourists. It is, therefore, advisable to plan a trip to Agra in advance especially during the winter months.

Arriving by Air

Agra airport (7 kms from the city centre) at Kheria has direct flights to and from Delhi and Varanasi. Flight schedules can be checked from your travel agent or from the airline offices listed below:

Airline Offices

Indian Airlines/ Alliance Air
Hotel Clarks Shiraz, 54 Taj Road
Ph 360948, 263116, Airport 301180-84

Jet Airways
Hotel Clarks Shiraz, 54 Taj Road
Ph 360303, 267944

Arriving by Train

Agra is well-connected by train to Delhi. The daily Shatabdi Express leaves New Delhi RS at 6 am and arrives at Agra Cantonment Railway Station at 7.55 am, giving the traveller adequate time to visit Taj Mahal and Agra Fort, before taking the evening Shatabdi Express back to Delhi at 8.10 pm to get to Delhi by 10.50 pm.

The other alternative is to board the daily Taj Express that leaves Nizamuddin RS in Delhi at 7.15 am to get into Agra Cantt at 9.45 am and leaves the city of the Taj at 6.25 pm to return to Delhi by 9.45 pm. There are also several other non-superfast trains to Agra.

Cars are available for hire at the airport and the railway station. With a good driver and an early start, it is possible to fit in Agra and Fatehpur Sikri (37 kms from Agra) in the same day. However, this would make for a very tight visit, and we would strongly recommend at least two days in Agra if you plan to visit Fatehpur Sikri.

Railway enquiry

Agra Cantt
Ph 131, Reservation 364519, 364131

Agra City
Ph 132, Reservation 364163

Arriving by Road

A four-lane highway connects Agra and Delhi. This road, National Highway 2, is one of the best maintained freeways in the country. The 204-km journey takes barely three hours by car. However, the traffic in Agra city itself is rather chaotic, and the few kilometres from the point of entering the city to the Taj or the Fort often takes over 30 minutes.

Road Distances from Agra		
Bharatpur	55	kms
Bhopal	541	kms
Fatehpur Sikri	37	kms
Gwalior	119	kms
Jaipur	240	kms
Khajuraho	400	kms
Lucknow	357	kms
Mathura	62	kms

By Bus

UP Roadways operates hourly bus services to Delhi, Jaipur and Mathura from the Idgah Bus Terminal. Frequent buses also leave for Fatehpur Sikri at gaps of half-an-hour.

Roadways enquiry

UP State Road Transport Corporation
Idgah Bus Stand, Ph 366124, 367543

Power House Bus Stand, Ph 364557

Rajasthan State Transport Corporation
Sheetal Tourist Home
Near Idgah Bus Stand, Ph 369420

Tourist Information Centres

UP Government Tourist Office
64 Raj Road, Ph 360517

UP Government Tourist Reception Counter
Agra Cantt, Ph 364439

Government of India Tourist Office
191 The Mall, Ph 363959, 363377

Where to shop

Agra is famous for inlay-work in marble and woollen carpets. The numerous small shops display an array of gold embroidered garments. Also available are purses and bags with *zardozi* or intricate hand embroidery done with gold and silver thread. Some of the major shopping centres are:

Gwalior Road

Kinari Bazar

Mahatma Gandhi Road

Pratap Pura

Sadar Bazar

Where to stay

Average rack-rate in rupees for a standard double room

A Above 6000 B 4000-6000 C 2500-4000
D 1500-2500 E Below 1500

A **Welcomgroup Mughal Sheraton**
Fatehabad Road
Ph 331701, 331702, Fax 331730

B **Agra Ashok**
6B Mall Road
Ph 361223, 361232, Fax 361620

B **Clarks Shiraz**
54 Taj Road, Ph 361421, Fax 361428

B **Mansingh Palace**
Fatehabad Road, Ph 33177, Fax 330202

B **Taj View**
Fatehabad Road, Taj Ganj
Ph 331841, 331859, Fax 331860

C **Jaypee Palace**
Fatehabad Road
Ph 330800, Fax 330850

C **Taj Khema** (UP Tourism)
East Gate of Taj Mahal, Ph 330140

D **Amar**
Fatehabad Road
Ph 331885, 331889, Fax 330299

D **Atithi**
Fatehabad Road, Ph 330879, 330884, Fax 30878

D **Grand**
137 Station Road, Agra Cantt
Ph 36404, 364311, Fax 364271

D **Ranjit**
263 Station Road, Agra Cantt
Ph 36446, Fax 364271

E **Tourist Bungalow** (UP Tourism)
Station Road, Raja ka Mandi
Ph 350120, 351720

At Fatehpur Sikri

Fatehpur Sikri is 37 kms away from Agra, and it is advisable to base yourself at Agra as accommodation is rather limited here.

D **Gulistan Tourist Bungalow**
(UP Tourism), Fatehpur Sikri
Ph 05619-2490

BHOPAL

STD Code : 0755

Sanchi Stupa

The nearest airport for Sanchi is at Bhopal, 46 kms away. Daily flights connect Bhopal with Delhi and Mumbai. Please check the flight schedules with the airline offices.

Airline Offices

Indian Airlines & Alliance Air
Airlines House, T T Nagar, Bhadbhada Road
Ph 778434, 770480

Airport Ph 521789, 521277

Air India
GTB Complex, T T Nagar, Ph 63468

Sahara India
3/195 M P Nagar, Zone 1
Ph 765242, Airport Ph 523768

Arriving by Train

Bhopal Railway Station is the nearest railhead for Sanchi and is well-connected by daily trains to Delhi, Mumbai, Agra and Chennai. From Delhi, it is best to take the superfast Shatabdi Express that leaves New Delhi RS at 6 am and arrives in Bhopal at 2.10 pm. It begins the return journey at 2.50 pm and arrives in Delhi at 10.50 pm.

Railway enquiry
General Enquiry : 131
Reservation 540170

Arriving by Road

Taxis can be hired from the airport or the railway station and it takes about an hour to reach Sanchi from Bhopal. The Madhya Pradesh Road Transport Corporation runs frequent deluxe as well as ordinary buses to Sanchi from the Hamidia Road Bus Stand.

MP Road Transport Corporation
Ph 540841

Road Distances from Bhopal

Agra	541 kms
Bhimbetka	40 kms
Gwalior	422 kms
Indore	187 kms
Kanha Sanctuary	540 kms
Khajuraho	387 kms
Pachmarhi	195 kms
Sanchi	46 kms

Tourist Information Offices

Madhya Pradesh Tourism Development Corporation
Gangotri Complex, Ph 554340, Fax 774289

Palash
(Near 45 Bungalows), T T Nagar
Ph 553006, 577440, Fax 553076

Where to stay

Average rack-rate in rupees for a standard double room

A Above 6000 B 4000-6000 C 2500-4000
D 1500-2500 E Below 1500

B **Jehan Numa Palace**
Simla Hills
Ph 540100, Fax 540720

B **Noor-Us-Sabah Palace**
VIP Road, Koh-e-Fiza
Ph 749101, Fax 749110

C **Lake View Ashok**
Simla Hills, Opposite TV Tower
Ph 541600, Fax 541606

C **Residency**
208 MP Nagar
Ph 556001, Fax 557637

D **Palash** (MP Tourism)
Near 45 Bungalows, T T Nagar
Ph 553006, Fax 552384

D **Amer Palace**
209, Zone 1, MP Nagar
Ph 272110, 272111, Fax 575308

D **Nisarga**
211, Zone 1, MP Nagar
Ph 555701, 555702, Fax 272701

E **Panchanan** (MP Tourism)
New Market, Ph 551647, Fax 552384

E **Ranjit**
3 Hamidia Road
Ph 534411, 535211, Fax 532242

At Sanchi

MP State Tourism Development Corporation runs a Travellers' Lodge at Sanchi. The latter provides clean but very basic facilities for those wishing to spend the night at Sanchi.

E **Travellers' Lodge**
Ph 07592-62723

KHAJURAHO

STD Code : 07686

Western Group of Temples

Arriving by Air

Khajuraho airport (5 kms from the Western Group of temples) has regular flights to Delhi. It would be best to check the flight timings either with your travel agent or from the airline offices listed below:

Airline offices

Jet Airways
Civil Aerodrome, Ph 44406, 440611

Indian Airlines
Hotel Temple Complex, Airport Road
Ph 74035, 74036

Arriving by Train

Jhansi Junction, 172 kms away, is the nearest railway station for Khajuraho. The New Delhi–Bhopal Shatabdi Express is the most convenient train to Jhansi. It leaves New Delhi RS at 6 am and gets into Jhansi at 10.25 am and the return train leaves Jhansi at 5.55 pm to reach Delhi by 10.50pm.

Satna (117 kms away) is the nearest railhead for travellers coming from Varanasi or Calcutta.

Arriving by Road

Khajuraho is connected by regular buses with Jhansi and Satna. The state roadways buses are available from outside Jhansi railway station.

Madhya Pradesh State Tourism Development Corporation
Chandela Cultural Centre, Ph 42330

Road Distances from Khajuraho

Agra	391	kms
Allahabad	120	kms
Bhopal	391	kms
Chitrakoot	69	kms
Jhansi	176	kms
Mahoba	50	kms
Panna National Park	58	kms
Raneh Falls	20	kms
Satna	117	kms

Where to shop

Shops near the Western Group of Temples sell stone and bronze sculptures, handicrafts and gems.

Where to stay

B **Holiday Inn**
Ph 44178, Fax 42304

B **Jass Oberoi**
Bypass Road, Ph 42344, 42366
Fax 42345

B **Taj Chandela**
Ph 42355, Fax 42366

C **Clarks Khajuraho**
Ph 44038, Fax 44257

C **Khajuraho Ashok**
Ph 44024, 44336, Fax 42239

D **Clarks Bundela**
Ph 42386, 42387, Fax 42385

D **Jhankar** (MP Tourism)
Airport Road, Ph 20634

D **Payal** (MP Tourism)
Ph 44064

E **Rahil** (MP Tourism)
Ph 44062

E **Tourist Village** (MP Tourism)
Ph 44128

MUMBAI

STD Code : 022

Elephanta • Ajanta • Ellora • Goa

Mumbai, earlier known as Bombay, is the commercial hub of India, and, therefore, extremely well connected by air and rail to most parts of India. In fact, for centuries, Mumbai has been an entry-point for those seeking India's splendours.

For the Heritage circuit, the cave temple of Elephanta is located on an island in the city harbour. Mumbai also allows easy access to Ajanta and Ellora, via Aurangabad, as well as to Goa.

Arriving by Air

Mumbai/Bombay airport, newly-renamed Chhatrapati Shivaji International Airport has two terminals, the international terminal at Sahar and the domestic terminal at Santa Cruz. Mumbai has almost hourly flights connecting it to Delhi, Chennai, Calcutta and Bangalore and at least one flight a day to Goa, Aurangabad and Bhopal. Please check the flight schedules with the airlines' offices listed below:

Airport Enquiry
International Terminal, Ph 8366700

Domestic Terminal, Ph 6113300, 6105923

Airline Offices

Air India
Air India Building, Nariman Point
Ph 2013031

Indian Airlines
Air India Building, Nariman Point
Ph 2023131, Airport Ph 6156633

Jet Airways
41-42 Maker Chamber 3, Nariman Point
Ph 2855788, Airport Ph 6156666

Sahara India
Unit 7, Ground floor, Tulsiani Chambers,
Nariman Point,
Ph 2835671, 2830752, Airport Ph 6156363

Arriving by Train

Mumbai has three main railway stations, namely Mumbai Central, Mumbai CST (formerly Victoria Terminus), and Dadar, that connect Mumbai to all major cities and towns of India. Daily trains leave Mumbai for Delhi, Chennai, Calcutta (Howrah), Bangalore and Goa (Madgaon).

Railway enquiry:
Train arrival/departure status

From the south: Ph 136
From the north: Ph 137

Tourist Information Centres

Government of India
123 Maharishi Karve Road
Ph 2033144, 2033145, Fax 2014496

Delhi Tourism Development Corporation
Ph 2856736

Goa Tourist Information Centre
Ph 3086288

India Tourism Development Corporation
Nirmal Building, 11th Floor, Nariman Point
Ph 2023343, 2026679, Fax 2880992

Madhya Pradesh State Tourism Development Corporation
Ph 2187603

Maharashtra Tourism Development Corporation
Opposite LIC Building, Madam Cama Road
Ph 2026713, 2067762

UP State Tourism Development Corporation
World Trade Centre, Cuffe Parade
Ph 2185458

Roadways Enquiry

BEST Transport
Ph 4143611, 4136883

Maharashtra State Road Transport
Maharashtra Vahatuk Bhavan
Dr Anand Rao Nair Marg, Ph 3071524

Traffic Control Room
Ph 4146162, 4146532

Accident Information
Mahim Ph 4451366
Sion Ph 4078653

Where to shop

Mumbai has an overwhelming array of things to buy. The southern part of the city has a string of upscale department stores like Benzer on Bhulabhai Desai Road. Visit Zaveri Bazar for jewellery and Fashion Street for bargains in ready-to-wear clothes. Also check out Colaba Causeway for almost everything under the sun.

Where to stay

Average rack-rate in rupees for a standard double room

A Above 6000 B 4000-6000 C 2500-4000
D 1500-2500 E Below 1500

A **Centaur**
Mumbai Airport
Ph 6156660, Fax 6156535

A **Centaur Juhu Beach**
Juhu Tara Road, Juhu Beach
Ph 6113040, Fax 6116343

A **Holiday Inn**
Balraj Sahani Marg, Juhu Beach
Ph 6904444, 6704444, Fax 6701710

A **Oberoi**
Nariman Point
Ph 2025757, Fax 2043282

A **Ramada Palm Grove**
Juhu Beach
Ph 6112323, 6147466, Fax 6110641

A **Taj Mahal**
Apollo Bunder, Colaba
Ph 2023366, Fax 2872711

B **Sun and Sand**
Juhu Beach,
Ph 6204821, 6204811 Fax 6202170

C **Citizen**
960 Juhu Beach
Ph 6117273, 6117766 Fax 6117170

C **Parle International**
Agarwal Market, Vile Parle East
Ph 6102122, 6102124, Fax 6128215

D **Ajanta**
8 Juhu Tara Road
Ph 6183047, 6183328, Fax 6177878

D **Apollo**
38 Garden Road, Colaba Causeway
Ph 2840020, 2872105, Fax 2874990

D **Juhu Continental**
Opposite Theosophical Society
Juhu Tara Road
Ph 6182563, 6182982, 6117503
Fax 6117502

Getting to Elephanta

The best time to visit Elephanta Cave is between November and March. Making the crossing in the monsoon months is best avoided.

There are regular launch services to Elephanta that leave every hour from the Gateway of India. On Sundays and public holidays the service is more frequent. The journey takes less than an hour and the cost is nominal. Maharashtra Tourism launches, with good guides on board, leave the Gateway of India every 30 minutes from 9 am. The last returns from Elephanta at 5.30 pm.

The climb from the jetty to the cave at Elephanta is fairly steep, so it is best to avoid the afternoon sun. You can also hire a carry-chair up the climb.

AURANGABAD

STD Code : 0240

Ajanta Caves • Ellora Caves

Ajanta and Ellora can be accessed from Aurangabad, a rapidly developing industrial town in the western Indian state of Maharashtra. Situated as it was on the arterial *dakshinapatha,* the ancient trade route to the South, it is a town steeped in history and is named for the Mughal emperor Aurangzeb.

Aurangabad is the starting point for the cave temples of Ajanta (106 kms) and Ellora (30 kms). It is well geared to meet tourist traffic and so is the most convenient place to stay while you visit the two sites.

Both sites are but a day's trip away, but do not attempt to cover both in the same day for they lie in different directions. Go to Aurangabad with two full days in hand. The trip to Ajanta will take up one full day and Ellora half-a-day, provided you don't take in Daulatabad.

Arriving by Air

Chikalthana airport is 10 kms from Aurangabad city and has direct daily flights to Delhi and Mumbai. The flight schedules can be checked with the airlines' offices listed below:

Airline Offices

Indian Airlines
Airlines House, Town Centre, Jalna Road
Ph 485012, 483392

Airport Ph 482111, 485780, 483390

Jet Airways
4 Santsheel, Vidya Nagar, Jalna Road
Ph 441770, 441392

Airport Ph 487071

Arriving by Train

Aurangabad is directly connected to Mumbai, Delhi, Agra, Goa and Bhopal. Alternatively, you can get a bus or train to the nearest mainline junction at Manmad, 113 km north-west of Aurangabad, from where there are a number of express trains to Mumbai and Delhi.

Arriving by Road

Aurangabad is connected by good roads to almost all major cities and towns. There are MSRTC buses from Aurangabad to Mumbai. MSRTC and ITDC also offer luxury overnight buses to Mumbai. It takes about 12 hours to reach Mumbai by bus.

There is a regular bus service from Aurangabad to the Ajanta caves, with the last bus leaving Ajanta at 5.45 pm.

Maharashtra State Road Transport Corporation (MSRTC)
Central Bus Stand, Mill Corner, Ph 331647

Important Road Distances

Bhopal	644 kms
Goa	712 kms
Mumbai	392 kms
Nanded	277 kms
Pune	229 kms
Shirdi	136 kms

Tours

MTDC, ITDC and MSRTC operate sightseeing tours to the caves at Ajanta and Ellora.

Ellora and city

Time	Reservation
Daily except Monday	**MSRTC** Central Bus Stand, Mill Corner Ph 331647

Ajanta Excursion

9.30 am to 6.00 pm Daily except Monday	**MTDC** Holiday Resort Station Road Ph 331513
8.00 am to 6.00 pm Daily except Monday	**MSRTC** Central Bus Stand, Mill Corner Ph 331647
9.30 am to 6.00 pm Daily except Monday	**MTDC** Holiday Resort Station Road Ph 331513

Tourist Information Centres

Government of India Tourist Office
Krishna Vilas, Station Road, Ph 331217

Maharashtra Tourism Development Corporation Limited (MTDC)
MTDC Holiday Resort, Station Road
Ph 331513, Fax 331198

Where to shop

Aurangabad is famous for Paithani silk, Himroo shawls and agate stones. The main shopping areas are City Chowk, Gulmandi and Shahganj.

Where to stay

Average rack-rate in rupees for a standard double room

A Above 6000 B 4000-6000 C 2500-4000
D 1500-2500 E Below 1500

B **Ambassador Ajanta**
Jalna Road, CIDCO Colony
Ph 85211, Fax 484367

B **Taj Residency**
8-N-12, CIDCO,
Ph 381106, 381107, Fax 381053

B **Welcomgroup Rama International**
R-3 Chikalthana
Ph 485441,485442, Fax 484768

D **MTDC Holiday Resort**
Station Road, Ph 34259

E **Amarpreet**
Jalna Road
Ph 332521, 332523, Fax 351346

E **Raviraj**
Dr Rajendra Prasad Marg, Ph 352124

At Ajanta

MTDC Holiday Resort
Ajanta Caves, Ph 02438-4226
(Only four, very basic rooms, but very well located)

MTDC Holiday Resort
Fardapur (5 kms from the Caves)
Ph 02438-4230

At Ellora

Basic accommodation is available at the following places:

Kailas
Ellora Caves
Ph 02437-44543, 02437-44446

Travellers' Bungalow
Khuldabad (3 kms from Ellora)
Ph 02437-22571

GOA

STD Code (Panjim) : 0832

Churches and Convents

The beaches of Goa have lured visitors for centuries, from the colonising Portuguese to the tourist today. But Goa has more to offer than just its beaches. The Portuguese convents and cathedrals of Old Goa (9 kms away from Panjim) are less than an hour's drive from the main beaches.

Goa could also be an alternative launch-pad to the temple towns of Hampi and Pattadakal in the neighbouring state of Karnataka. Both Hampi, the capital of the medieval empire of Vijayanagar, and the much smaller Pattadakal are best accessed from the base town of Hospet, which is a 10-hour drive eastwards from Goa. Taxis are easily available.

Arriving by Air

Goa's international airport, Dabolim is 27 kms from Panjim. All the major Indian domestic airlines operate here. There are daily direct flights from Goa to Delhi, Mumbai, and Bangalore and a bi-weekly one to Chennai. It is best to check flight timings with the airline offices listed below:

Airline Offices

Indian Airlines
Dempo House, Campal, Panjim
Ph 223831, 224067, 227826

Airport Ph 513863

Air India
Hotel Fidalgo, Ground Floor, 1st June Road, Panjim, Ph 231101, 225172

Airport Ph 513445

Jet Airways
Sesa Ghor, Shop Nos 7, 8, & 9, Patto Plaza, Panjim
Ph 221472, 221476

Airport Ph 510354

Sahara India
Shop No 1, 2, 3, Ground Floor, Live-in-Apartments, General Benad Guides Road, Panjim
Ph 226291, 230634, 237346

Airport Ph 510043

Arriving by Rail

The nearest railheads are Vasco de Gama, 30 kms from Panjim and Madgaon, 33 kms from Panjim. Goa is also serviced by Londa junction (192 kms from Vasco) that is on the mainline south to Bangalore. There are daily trains to and from Delhi and Mumbai from Madgaon.

Arriving by Road

Goa is connected to Bangalore, Mumbai, Pune, Mangalore and other major towns in neighbouring states. There are daily bus services from Panjim, Mapusa and Margao for Bangalore, Mangalore, Mumbai, and Pune. Karnataka and Maharashtra State Road Transport Corporation buses also operate from Goa.

Goa's Kadamba Transport Corporation (KTC) operates luxury and ordinary buses to Old Goa, Mapusa, Margao, Vasco, Ponda and Calangute.

Kadamba Transport Corporation of Goa, as well as Karnataka State Road Transport Corporation run daily overnight buses from Panjim to Hampi, as do some private bus operators. Buses to Badami, the town closest to Pattadakal, are less reliable, and it is best to hire a taxi.

Motorcycles are available on rent for moving around the town and insurance cover is provided to the customers. An international driving licence is required to drive these motorcycles. Bicycles can also be rented in Goa at nominal rates. They are ideal for moving around the city, although going to Old Goa from any of the beaches is probably a longish ride.

Road Distances from Panjim

Aurangabad	712 kms
Badami	312 kms
Bangalore	598 kms
Hampi	323 kms
Hospet	350 kms
Hubli	184 kms
Mumbai	594 kms
Pattadakal	489 kms
Pune	458 kms

Tourist Offices

Government of India Tourist Office
Communidade Building, Church Square
Ph 243412

Government of Goa
Tourist Home, Panjim
Ph 224757, Fax 228819

Government of Karnataka
Velhos Building, Panjim, Ph 224110

Tours

Goa Tourism Development Corporation (GTDC) organises conducted tours to Old Goa from Tourist Hotel, Panjim, Ph 227103, 223396. Excellent guides are available at Old Goa who take you through the Convents and Churches.

Where to shop

Goa's bustling shopping district at Panjim has nothing special to offer that is not available in any other Indian city. What the tourist must look for are the fried and spiced cashewnuts and the local brew, feni, made either from cashewnut or coconut. The flea market at Anjuna Beach, 22 kms from Panjim, is a charming place to search for bargains.

Where to stay

Being a popular tourist destination, Goa has an extremely wide range of accommodation. Given below are a few establishments.

Average rack-rate in rupees for a standard double room

A Above 6000 B 4000-6000 C 2500-4000
D 1500-2500 E Below 1500

A **Cidade De Goa**
Vainguinim Beach
Ph 221133, Fax 223303

A **Holiday Inn Resort Goa**
Mobor Beach, Cavelossim
Ph 746303, Fax 746333

A **Fort Aguada Beach Resort**
Sinquerim, Bardez
Ph 276201, Fax 276044

A **Leela Palace Goa**
Mobor, Cavelossim
Ph 746363, Fax 746352

B **Majorda Beach Resort**
Majorda, Salcete
Ph 754871, Fax 755382, 754342

B **Ronil Royale**
Baga Road, Ph 276101, Fax 276068

C **Mandovi**
D B Bandodkar Marg
Ph 224405, Fax 225451

D **Fidalgo**
18th June Road, Ph 226291

D **Baia Do Sol**
Baga Beach, Ph 276084, Fax 731415

D **Concha Beach Resort**
Utur Waddo, Calangute Beach, Bardez
Ph 276056, Fax 276056

D **Kamat Holiday Homes**
Near St Anthony's Chapel,
Calangute, Bardez
Ph 277009, 277226, Fax 276545

E **Delmon**
Caetano de Albuquerque Road
Ph 226846, 226847, 226848

E **Rukmini**
D D Road, Near MPT Hall,
Vasco Da Gama,
Ph 512350, 511784, Fax 511785

E **La Pez Gardens**
Swantatra Path, Vasco De Gama
Ph 512121, 512122, Fax 513302

Beaches in North Goa

	Distance from Panjim
Anjuna	22 kms
Baga	18 kms
Candolim	12 kms
Calangute	16 kms
Sinquerim	13 kms
Vagator	24 kms

Beaches in South Goa

	Distance from Panjim
Bambolim	10 kms
Benaulim	41 kms
Bogmalo	21 kms
Cavelossim	50 kms
Colva	39 kms
Dona Paula	7 kms
Palolem	80 kms

BANGALORE

STD Code : 080

Pattadakal • Hampi

Bangalore was a salubrious colonial town until it jetted into the future, riding the IT revolution. Today, it is India's answer to Silicon Valley, with most hi-tech corporations based here. Cosmopolitan in flavour, it is the ideal place to access the Heritage sites of Hampi and Pattadakal.

Both the temple towns, however, are an immense distance away to the North – Hampi is 353 kms away and Pattadakal 514 kms – and reaching them entails practically a whole day's driving. Thankfully the roads are reasonably good, especially up to Hospet, from where it is possible to make day trips to both sites.

Arriving by Air

Bangalore airport is 7.5 kms away from the city centre on MG road and is connected by daily flights to Delhi, Mumbai, Goa, Chennai and Calcutta. Please check the flight schedules with the airline offices listed below:

Airline Offices

Indian Airlines
Cauvery Bhawan, Kempegowda Road
Ph 2211914

Airport Ph 5266233

Air India
Unity Buildings, JC Road
Ph 227774, 227754

Airport Ph 5261531

Jet Airways
1-4 M Block, Unity Building, JC Road
Ph 2276620, Airport Ph 5266898, 5261926

Sahara
Unit G-2 Church Gate, 35 Church Street
Ph 5584457

Airport Ph 5271286

Arriving by Train

Bangalore railway station is located near Gandhi Nagar. Bangalore is connected by rail to Delhi, Mumbai, Chennai and other major cities.

Railway Enquiry
General Ph 131

Reservations Ph 132, 2876464

Arrivals/Departures Ph 133

Arriving by Road

Karnataka State Transport Corporation buses are available to Hampi, Pattadakal, Belgaum, Hospet and other tourist destinations in Karnataka, from Inter-State Bus Station or Central Bus Station, just opposite the Bangalore City Railway Station.

Roadways Enquiry

Inter State Bus Station
Ph 2871261

Karnataka State Road Transport Corpn
Ph 2873377

Tamil Nadu State Road Transport Corpn
Ph 2863637

Goa Road Transport Corpn (C/o KSRTC)
Ph 2873377

Tourist Information Offices

Karnataka State Tourism
No.10/4 Kasturba Road, Ph 2212901-03

City Railway Station Counter Ph 2870068

Airport Ph 5268012

Karnataka State Tourist Office
Badami House, NR Square
Ph 2275869, 2275883

Karnataka State Tourist Office
1st floor, F Block, Cauvery Bhawan
Ph 2215489 Fax 2272403

Karnataka Darshini
64 St Marks Road, Ph 2236854

Government of India Tourist Office
KFC Building, 48 Church Street, Ph 5585417

Tamil Nadu Tourist Information Centre
Ph 2286181

Where to stay

Average rack-rate in rupees for a standard double room

A Above 6000 B 4000-6000 C 2500-4000
D 1500-2500 E Below 1500

A **Taj West End**
Race Course Road
Ph 2255055, Fax 2200010

A **Windsor Manor**
25 Sankey Road
Ph 2269898, Fax 2264941

B Le Meridien
28 Sankey Road
Ph 2262233, Fax 2267676

B Taj Residency
41/3 Mahatma Gandhi Road
Ph 5584444, Fax 5584748

B Central Park
47 Dickenson Road, Manipal Centre
Ph 5584242, Fax 5588594

C Samrat Residency
173/1 SC Road
Ph 3360822, Fax 3465657

D Quality Inn Kensington Terrace
14/7 Mahatma Gandhi Road
Ph 5594666, Fax 5594029

E Mahaveer
Near City Railway Station
Ph 2870741, Fax 2870735

E Nilgiri Nest
171 Brigade Road
Ph 5588702, Fax 5585348

PATTADAKAL

Arriving by Air

Bangalore (514 kms) is the nearest airport. On arrival at Bangalore airport, you can hire a taxi to reach Pattadakal but the drive could easily take about 11-12 hours.

Arriving by Train

Gadag (96 kms) is the nearest junction connecting Pattadakal to Bangalore. The most convenient train to take is the daily Bangalore-Hampi Express that leaves Bangalore at 10 pm and reaches Gadag at 9.25 am the next day. For the return trip, it leaves Gadag station at 6 pm to get into Bangalore by 6.25 am.

Arriving by Road

State run buses are available from Bangalore to Badami (485 kms). Pattadakal is only 29 kms from Badami. You can use Badami as the base for Pattadakal as there are no hotels in Pattadakal. There are only a couple of shacks outside the temple complex selling tender coconuts and aerated drinks. The visitor is, hence, advised to stay in Badami, which has a number of reasonable hotels.

The other alternative is to stay at Aihole, another temple town 21 kms from Pattadakal. At Aihole you can stay at the Tourist Home operated by KSTDC, Ph 08351-34541. This hotel has basic facilities but is clean and has a restaurant. The nearest police station is at Badami or at Amingad, 9 kms further from Aihole.

Where to stay

At Badami

B Badami Court
17/3 Station Road
Ph 08357-65230, Fax 08357-65207

D Mukambika Deluxe
Opposite Bus Stand

E Mayura Chalukya
Ramadurg Road, Ph 08357- 65046

HAMPI

STD Code : 08394

Arriving by Air

Bangalore (353 kms) is the nearest airport. The easiest way to reach Hampi is by hiring a taxi directly from the airport. You can also take a tourist bus to Hampi, or a train to Hospet, 13 kms away.

Arriving by Train

Hospet is the nearest and most convenient railhead and is connected to Bangalore by a daily overnight train, the Bangalore-Hampi Express that leaves Bangalore at 10 pm and gets into Hospet at 7.50 am the next morning. For the return journey, it leaves Hospet at 8.10 pm and reaches Bangalore by 6.25 am the next day.

Arriving by Road

The Karnataka State Road Transport Corporation (KSRTC) bus stand is just opposite the railway station. KSRTC operates frequent services to Hospet (340 kms) and Hampi (353 kms). You can base yourself at Hospet to visit Hampi. It is used as a base by many tourists as it offers a wider choice of accommodation.

Where to stay

At Hospet

C Malligi
6/143 J N Road,
Ph 08394-28101, Fax 08394-27038

D Priyadarshani
Station Road, Ph 08394-28838

E Mayura Vijayanagar
Tungabhadra Dam, Ph 08394-59270

At Hampi

E Mayura Bhuvaneshwari
Kamalapur Village
Ph 51374

CHENNAI

STD Code : 044

Thanjavur • Mamallapuram

Chennai, the capital of the state of Tamil Nadu. An important commercial and cultural centre for South India, it is also the entry point for two World Heritage sites, the rock temples of Mamallapuram (58 kms) and the Brihadisvara Temple at Thanjavur (334 kms).

Arriving by Air

Chennai has an international airport, the Aringar Anna International Airport. This terminal – as well as the domestic one, the Kamraj Domestic Airport – is at Meenambakkam, 12 kms from the city centre. Chennai is connected by daily flights to Delhi, Bangalore, Calcutta and Mumbai. Please check flight schedules from the airline offices listed below.

Airport enquiry
General enquiry Ph 140

Flight arrival Ph142, 5119433, 5119437

Flight Departure Ph 142, 5119841, 5119844

Airline Offices

Indian Airlines
19 Rukmani Lakshmipathy Road, Egmore
Ph 8553039, 8555200

Airport Ph 2344433, 2343131

Air India
19 Rukmani Lakshmipathy Road, Egmore
Ph 8554477, 8554488

Airport Ph 2344927, 2347500, 2347400

Jet Airways
Thapar House, 43/44 Montieth Road, Egmore, Ph 8555109

Airport Ph 2328080, 2346728

Sahara India
4&5 Lokesh Towers
18 Kodambakkam High Road
Ph 8263661, 8271961

Airport Ph 2311542, 2311543

Arriving by Train

Chennai has two main railway stations, Egmore station for trains to towns in the southern region, and Chennai Central for trains to other parts of the country. Chennai is connected by daily trains to Delhi, Bhopal, Bangalore, Mumbai and Calcutta.

Arrival/Departure from Central and Egmore
Ph 5357583

Arrival/Departure (South), Ph 134 (Egmore)

Arrival/Departure (North), Ph 133
(Chennai Central)

Arriving by Road

Buses run by the state-owned Tamil Nadu Transport Corporation originate from the main bus stand at Esplanade. The Interstate Bus Depot at Broadway handles enquiries and reservation for long-distance journeys.

Roadways Enquiry

Tamil Nadu State Express Transport
Ph 5341836, 5341835

Andhra Pradesh State Road Transport Corporation
Ph 5342122

Karnataka State Road Transport Corporation
Ph 5340449

Tourist Information Offices

Goverment of India Tourist Information Office
154 Anna Salai, Ph 8524785, 8524295

Airport Ph 2340386

India Tourism Development Corporation
29 Victoria Crescent
Commander-in-Chief Road, Egmore
Ph 8278884, 8244216

Orissa Tourism Information Centre
Ph 8534090

Tamil Nadu Tourist Office
735 Anna Salai, Ph 8514850

Tamil Nadu Tourist Information Office
Kamaraj Domestic Terminal
Ph 2340569

Central Railway Station, Ph 5353351

Egmore Railway Station, Ph 8252165

Tamil Nadu Tourism Development Corporation
25 Dr Radhakrishnan Salai, Mylapore
Ph 8547344, 8547346

Tirupati-Thirumalai Devasthanam Information Centre
Ph 4993879, 4343535

Uttar Pradesh Tourism Office
Ph 8283276

West Bengal Information Bureau
18 Wallajah Road, Ph 8532346

Tours & Travels

Ashok Travels
Ph 8553205

Mercury Travels
Ph 8522993

Sita World Travels
Ph 8278861

Thomas Cook
Ph 8554600

Travel Corporation of India
Ph 8523013

Guided Tours

Tamil Nadu Tourism Development Corporation conducts guided tours in and around Chennai. Advance bookings can be made at:

TTDC Sales Counter
Express Bus Stand, Ph 5341982

Tamil Nadu Tourist Information Centre
Central Railway Station, Ph 5353351

Egmore Railway Station, Ph 8252165

Airport, Ph 2340569

TTDC Sales Counter
New Delhi, Ph 3363607, 3365358

TTDC Sales Counter
Calcutta, Ph 4720432, 4729611

Bookshops

Giggles
Taj Connemara, Binny Road, Ph 8520123

Higginbothams
814 Anna Salai, Ph 8522420

Landmark
Apex Plaza, 3 NH Road, Ph 8279637

Where to shop

Chennai is known for its silks and its statues of bronze. The city's principal shopping areas are T Nagar and Anna Salai. T Nagar's Pondy Bazaar is dazzling in its variety and colour and Chennai's famous saree shops, Nalli's and Kumaran's, are both here, as are numerous other silk and jewellery shops. The Victoria Technical Institute at Anna Salai is the best place to pick up bronze items.

The other places for South Indian handicrafts are the Central Cottage Industries and Poompuhar, both at Anna Salai. Spencer's Plaza at Anna Salai is a famous all-you-need department store.

Where to stay

Average rack-rate in rupees for a standard double room

A Above 6000 B 4000-6000 C 2500-4000
D 1500-2500 E Below 1500

A **Taj Coromandel**
17 MG Road, Nungambakkam
Ph 8272827, Fax 8257104

A **Taj Connemara**
Binny Road, Ph 8520123, Fax 8523361

A **Trident**
GST Road, Ph 2344747, Fax 2346699

A **Welcomgroup Chola Sheraton**
10 Cathedral Road
Ph 8280101, Fax 8280101

A **Welcomgroup Park Sheraton Hotel and Towers**
TTK Road, Ph 4994101, Fax 4997101

C **Savera**
69 Dr Radhakrishnan Salai, Mylapore
Ph 8274700, Fax 8273475

C **Quality Inn Aruna**
144 Sterling Road, Nungambakkam
Ph 8259090, Fax 8258282

D **Residency**
49 G N Chetty Road, T Nagar
Ph 8253434, Fax 8250085

D **Sindoori Central**
26/27 Poonamallee High Road
Ph 5386647, 8295838, Fax 5387022

E **Chandra Towers**
9 Gandhi Road, Egmore
Ph 8233344, Fax 8251703

THANJAVUR

STD Code : 04362

Thanjavur was the heart of the Chola empire in the 8th-10th century AD. A town that bears its traditions with pride, Thanjavur is redolent with atmosphere.

The best way to see the Brihadisvara Temple is to base yourself at Thiruchirapalli, 54 kms away. Not only is Trichy, as the town is commonly known, a bigger city, it also has an airport. Even if you are coming in from Chennai by rail, it is preferable to take the train to Trichy which is faster and more frequent. From Trichy, Thanjavur is less than a two-hour drive away.

Arriving by Air

There are daily flights from Chennai to Thiruchirapalli, but please check the schedules at the Trichy number given here.

Indian Airlines
City Office Ph 0431-462233, 463930
Airport Ph 0431-420563

Arriving by Road

From Thiruchirapalli, you can hire a taxi for Thanjavur or else take a bus from the state transport bus stand. There are regular buses from Trichy for Thanjavur every 15 to 20 minutes. The fare is Rs 12 and it takes about 1 hour and 45 minutes to reach Thanjavur.

The bus stand is 1 km away from Trichy railway station. Buses also leave from the Central Bus Station and from Chinthamani-Main Guard Gate Bus Stand.

Roadways Enquiry – Thiruchirapalli
Ph 0431-460420, 0431-460992

Arriving by Train

Thanjavur has a railway station 8 kms away from the city centre. Direct trains are available to Chennai (Egmore), Bangalore and Mysore. However, it might be better to take a train to Trichy which is situated on the mainline and hence connected daily to Chennai and Bangalore.

From Chennai, for instance, the Rock Fort Express, is a superfast train that leaves Egmore at 10 pm and gets in to Trichy at 5.15 am the next day. The return train starts at 10 pm and gets into Egmore station at 5.20 am the next morning.

Where to stay

At Thanjavur

- D **Parisutham**
  55 GA, Canal Road, Ph 21844
- D **Sangam**
  Trichy Road, Ph 25151, 25026
- D **Tamil Nadu (TTDC)**
  Gandhiji Road, Ph 21421, 21024, 21325

At Thiruchirapalli

- B **Sangam**
  Collector's Office Road
  Ph 0431-414700, 414480
- D **Fortune Hotel Jenneys Residency**
  Mcdonald's Road
  Ph 0431-414414, Fax 461451
- E **Royal Southern**
  Race Course Road
  Khajamalai, Ph 0431-421307

Tourist Information Centre

Tourist office
1 Williams Road, Cantonment
Ph 460136

MAMALLAPURAM

STD Code : 04113

The ancient town of Mamallapuram, 58 kms south of Chennai was a thriving port of the Pallava dynasty during the 7th-8th centuries. Today it is famous for its many rock-cut temples, as well as the Shore Temple.

Arriving by Air

Chennai's Kamraj domestic terminal (64 kms) is the nearest airport.

Arriving by Train

Chengalpet (29 kms) is the nearest railway station. This is on the main line from Chennai and Kanchipuram and is serviced by daily trains. You can get either a TN State Transport bus or a taxi to Mamallapuram from Chengalpet.

Arriving by Road

To proceed to Mamallapuram, one can hire a taxi from the airport. The Tamil Nadu Tourist Information counter at the airport also arranges a coach service to the city centre, Parry's Corner, from where you can get a Tamil Nadu State Transport Corporation bus to Mamallapuram, an hour's drive away.

Tourist Information

Government of Tamil Nadu Tourist Office
Ph 42232

Where to stay

- A **Fisherman's Cove**
  Covelong Beach, Chengalpet
  Ph 74301, 74310
- C **Silver Sands**
  Covelong Road, Ph 42228
- C **Temple Bay Ashok Beach Resort**
  ITDC Shore Cottage
  Ph 42251, 42252, Fax 42257
- D **Golden Sun Hotel and Beach Resort**
  59 Covelong Road
  Ph 42245, Fax 4982669
- D **Tamil Nadu (TTDC)**
  Beach Resort Complex,
  Ph 42235, 42361

Road Distances from Chennai

Kanyakumari	700 kms
Madurai	447 kms
Ooty	565 kms
Tirupati	150 kms

BHUBANESHWAR

STD Code : 0674

Konarak Sun Temple

Bhubaneshwar is the capital of the eastern Indian state of Orissa. It is the entry point to visit the famous Sun Temple at Konarak (65 kms), and itself houses the beautiful Lingaraja Temple. The beautiful seaside resort of Puri (35 kms) is also a possible day-trip from Bhubaneshwar.

Arriving by Air

Bhubaneshwar airport is located 4 kms from the city. There are direct flights to Bhubaneshwar from Calcutta, Chennai, Delhi and Mumbai. Flight details can be checked from the airline offices or your travel agent.

Airline Offices

Indian Airlines/ Alliance Air
VII-C/8, Rajpath Unit I
Ph 530533, 530544

Airport Ph 406472, 401084

Arriving by Train

Bhubaneswar is connected by daily trains to Delhi, Calcutta, Chennai and Mumbai and twice a week to Bangalore.

Arriving by Road

The new bus terminal is located at Baramunda 6 kms away from the centre of the town. Buses for Konarak, Calcutta, Cuttack and the seaside resort of Puri depart from this terminal. Taxis are freely available to make the trip to Konarak, an hour-and-a-half away.

Tourist Information Centres

Government of India Tourist Office
B/21 BJB Nagar, Ph 432203

Orissa Tourist Office
Jayadev Marg, Ph 431299

Airport counter, Ph 404006

Railway Station counter, Ph 404715

Orissa Tourist Office, Puri
VIP Chowk, Station Road, Puri
Ph 06752-22664

Orissa Tourist Office, Konarak
Yatri Niwas, Ph 06758-35821

Where to shop

Orissa is famous for *ikat* fabrics, applique work and the *Patachitra* paintings of Raghurajpur. Its silver filigree work and carvings in stone and wood are also justly famed. These handicrafts can be bought at the market off Rajpath or from Orissa State Handloom Cooperative or Utalika Emporium and the Orissa State Handicrafts Emporium.

Where to stay

Average rack-rate in rupees for a standard double room

A Above 6000 B 4000-6000 C 2500-4000
D 1500-2500 E Below 1500

A **Oberoi Bhubaneshwar**
Naya Palli, Ph 440890, Fax 440898

C **Kalinga Ashok**
Gautam Nagar,
Ph 431055, 431056, Fax 432066

C **Swosti**
103 Janpath
Ph 518253, 518260, Fax 507524

D **Panthnivas**
Lewis Road
Ph 54115, 55314, Fax 403677

D **Prachi**
6 Janpath
Ph 502328, 502689, Fax 503287

E **Siddhartha**
A/19 Cuttack Road
Ph 575981, 579982, Fax 575985

E **Keshari**
113 Station Square
Ph 521994, 521995, Fax 511553

At Konarak

D **Yatrinivas (OTDC)**
Ph 06758-35820

D **Panthnivas**
Ph 06758-35831

D **Travellers' Lodge (OTDC)**
Ph 06758-35823

D **Inspection Bungalow (PWD)**
Ph 06758-35834

DARJEELING

STD Code : 0354

Darjeeling Himalayan Railway

The enchanting hill resort of Darjeeling is located in the northern part of the Indian state of West Bengal. The majestic view of Himalayan range, ruled by Kanchenjunga, the third-highest mountain peak in the world; the hills greened by pines and ferns; tea gardens on the slopes; streams, waterfalls and lakes; white magnolias and the red rhododendrons have all worked to make this town the queen of hill stations.

Arriving by Air

Bagdogra (90 kms from Darjeeling) is the nearest airport and is connected to Delhi, Calcutta and Guwahati with direct flights. From Bagdogra one can take a taxi or a bus to Siliguri (11 kms) which is the principal transit point for the Darjeeling Hills.

Airline Offices

Jet Airways
Stephen Court, 18D Park Street, Calcutta
Ph 033-2292227

Airport Ph 033-5119894

Indian Airlines
Airlines House, 39 Chittaranjan Avenue, Calcutta, Ph 033-2360730

Airport Ph 033-5119637

Jet Airways
Hotel Vinayak, Hill Cart Road, Siliguri
Ph 0353-435876, 435877

Bagdogra Airport Ph 03556-551588, 551590

Indian Airlines
Hotel Vinayak, Hill Cart Road, Siliguri
Ph 0353-431509

Bagdogra Airport Ph 03556-551666

Arriving by Train

The nearest major railway station for Darjeeling is New Jalpaiguri (82 kms) which is connected to most major cities. New Jalpaiguri is also the station from where 'Toy Train' to Darjeeling begins its romantic journey.

Arriving by Road

By road, Darjeeling is about 686 kms from Calcutta. There are regular bus services from Calcutta to Siliguri (606 kms away).

Tourist Information Centres

West Bengal Tourist Information Centre
1, Nehru Road, Darjeeling
Ph 54050

Hill Cart Road, Siliguri
Ph 0353-431974, 0353-441979

Where to shop

You can pick up local handicrafts like hand-painted *tankhas*, hand-woven cloth,carpets, jewellery and curios from numerous shops at Chowrasta and Chowk Bazar.

Where to stay

Average rack-rate in rupees for a standard double room

A Above 6000 B 4000-6000 C 2500-4000
D 1500-2500 E Below 1500

A **Windamere**
Observatory Hill
Ph 54041, 54042,
Fax 54043, 54211

C **Mohit**
Mount Pleasant Road
Ph 54723, 54818, Fax 54351

C **Sinclair**
18/1, Gandhi Road
Ph 3431, 3432, Fax 54355

D **New Elgin**
H D Lama Road
Ph 54114, Fax 54267

D **WBTDC Tourist Lodge**
Bhanu Sarani
Ph 54411, 54412

E **Apsara**
Ladenla Road
Ph 52983, 56285, Fax 54484

FURTHER READING

Aiyar, P V Jagdisa, *South Indian Shrines* (Delhi, 2000).

Archaeological Survey of India, *Archaeological Remains:* Monuments & Museums, Parts I & II (Delhi,1996).

Behl, Benoy K, *The Ajanta Caves: Ancient Paintings of Buddhist India* (London, 1998).

Blake, S P, *Shahjahanabad: The Sovereign City in Mughal India, 1639-1739* (Delhi, 1993).

Brown, Percy, *Indian Architecture: Buddhist and Hindu* (Bombay, 1996).

Coomaraswamy, Ananda, *History of Indian and Indonesian Art* (New York, 1988).

Devakunjari, D, *Hampi* (Delhi,1998).

Fergusson, James and Burgess, J A S, *The Cave Temples of India* (London, 1880).

Gupte, R S, *The Iconography of the Buddhist Sculptures of Ellora* (Aurangabad, 1964).

Harle, J C, *The Art and Architecture of the Indian Subcontinent* (New Haven, 1994).

Kail, Owen, C, *Elephanta: The Island of Mystery* (Bombay, 1984).

Kaye M M (ed), *The Golden Calm* (New York, 1980).

Keay, John, *History of India* (Delhi, 2000).

Kramrisch, Stella, *The Presence of Shiva* (Princeton, 1981).

Longhurst, A H, *Hampi Ruins* (Madras,1917; Reprint Delhi,1999).

Mansingh, Surjit, *Historical Dictionary of India* (Delhi, 1998).

Meister, Michael W and Dhaky M A (ed) *Encyclopaedia of Indian Temple Architecture, South India* (Philadelphia, 1986).

Mitra, Debala, *Sanchi* (Delhi,1992).

Mitra, Debala, *Ajanta* (Delhi, 1996).

Mitra, Debala, *Konarak* (Delhi, 1998).

Morris, Jan, *The Spectacle of Empire* (London, 1982).

National Council for Educational Research and Training (NCERT), *Ancient India* (Delhi, 2000).

NCERT, *Medieval India* (Delhi, 2000).

O'Flaherty, W, *Elephanta: The Cave of Shiva* (Delhi, 1983).

Rajgopalan, S, *Old Goa* (Delhi, 1984).

Rizvi, Sayid Athar Abbas, *Fatehpur Sikri* (New Delhi, 1992).

Sewell, Robert, *A Forgotten Empire: Vijayanagar* (London, 1900; Reprint Delhi, 1991).

Sharma, Y D, *Delhi and its Neighbourhood* (Delhi, 1990).

Sivamurti, C, *The Chola Temples* (Delhi, 1992).

Spear, Percival (Annotated by Narayani Gupta & Laura Sykes), *Delhi: Its Monuments and History* (Delhi, 1994).

Thapar, Romila & Spear, Percival, *Penguin History of India, Vols I & II* (Hammondsworth, 1966).

Tillotson, G H R, *Mughal India* (London, 1990).

GUIDEBOOKS

Abram, David, *Goa: The Rough Guide* (London,1999).

Bradnock, Robert and Roma, *India Handbook* (Bath, 2000).

Dorling Kindersley Travel Guides, *Delhi, Agra & Jaipur* (London, 2000).

Eicher City Guide, *Delhi* (Delhi, 1998).

Eicher City Map, *Delhi* (Delhi, 2001).

Eicher Travel Guide, *Walking With The Buddha: Buddhist Pilgrimages in India* (Delhi 1999).

Lonely Planet Travel Guide, *India* (Hawthorn, 1999).

Lonely Planet City Guide, *Delhi* (Hawthorn 1996).

Nicholson, Louise, *Delhi, Agra and Jaipur: India's Golden Triangle* (Hong Kong, 1996).

GLOSSARY

adisthana stone base of a temple
antarala vestibule in front of shrine
apsara celestial nymph
architrave beam extending from column to column
ardhmandapa compartment in front of main hall of temple
Ardhnarishwara Shiva as half-man, half-woman
Arjuna third of the five Pandava brothers, heroes of the epic *Mahabharata*; epitome of valour
artha wealth
baoli step well
basti shantytown
begum high-ranking Muslim lady
bhakta devotee
Bhima the second Pandava brother; epitome of strength
bhoga mandapa temple hall where offerings of food are made to the gods (Orissa)
bhulbhulaiyan labyrinth
Boddhisattava the ideal of Mahayana Buddhism; an individual who delays his own Enlightenment in order to lead other sentient beings to deliverance
Brahma one of the holy Trinity in the Hindu pantheon; attributed with the power of creating the cosmos
Brahmin/Brahman the priestly caste: the highest in the Hindu caste hierarchy
chaitya Buddhist hall of worship
charbagh *char*, four and *bagh*, garden; the classical Persian manner of laying gardens, with water channels dividing a larger garden into four smaller ones
chaturstala four-storeyed
chhajja eaves or portion of the roof projecting beyond the walls
chhatraveli the triple umbrella sacred to Buddhists, representing the Buddha, Dharma and Sangha
chhatri domed and pillared kiosk
corbel blocks of stone projecting from a wall: bracket
cruciform in the shape of a cross
cupola spherical roof
dakshinapatha southern route

dargah shrine of a Sufi saint
darwaza gate, door
deul temple (Orissa, Bengal)
deva gods in Hindu mythology
devadasis hand maidens to the gods; dancing girls in temples
Dharma translated variously as natural law, the truth; the teaching of the enlightened ones; moral or religious duty, decreed by law or custom
dhwajastambha flagstaff
Diwan-i-Am Hall of Public Audience
Diwan-i-Khas Hall of Private Audience
Draupadi shared wife of the five Pandava brothers of *Mahabharata*
dwarapala doorkeeper
finial uppermost portion of a pinnacle
firman diktat
fluting vertical channels on the shaft of a column
gana a dwarfish, impudent member of the host of minor deities who are followers of Shiva
Ganesha the elephant-headed son of Parvati and Shiva, worshipped as the god of auspicious beginnings
garbhagriha sanctum sanctotum or most sacred part of a shrine
gopuram monumental gateway in South Indian temples
Hari another name for Vishnu
haveli mansion
iwan prominent central arch of a mosque or tomb
jagamohana assembly hall in temple (Orissa)
jali net; intricate lattice work on marble or stone screen
Jataka the 547 Jatakas or Birth Stories are allegorical tales relating to the Buddha's previous births
jharokha small balcony with columns supporting a hood
jyotirlinga *linga* of light, one of the twelve said to be most sacred
kalasha vase; ornamental pot on finials and capitals of temples
kalyana mandapa wedding hall in temples (South India); pavillion where the marriage of the deity is ritually celebrated
kalyanasundaram the auspicious wedding of Shiva and Parvati: the subject of countless sculptures and friezes
Krishna most charming and accessible of all Hindu gods; as eighth avatar of Vishnu he came to earth to combat evil; the cow-herd god of love
Lakshmi goddess of wealth
linga phallus; aniconic symbol of Shiva
Mahabharata one of the two Hindu epics; ascribed to the poet Vyasa
mahamandapa great hall of a temple
Mahishasurmardini another name of Durga, the goddess of war; slayer of Mahishasura, the buffalo-demon
mandapa assembly hall attached to the sanctum of a temple
mandir temple
mardana men's quarters
masjid mosque
mihrab a recess in the mosque marking the direction of the Ka'aba in Mecca
mimar-i-kul architect-in-chief
mithuna loving couples
muqarnas a Persian architectural technique of holding up a structure like a balcony with a web of tiny arches
Nandi Shiva's vehicle, the sacred bull
Nataraja Lord of Dance; another name of Shiva
natya mandir dancing hall
navagraha nine planets
panchayatna temple with five shrines
parivara devatas family deities
parivaralaya tutelary shrines in Dravida temples
Parvati daughter of Himalaya; consort of Shiva
pietra dura inlay of precious stone in marble background
pilaster square pillar projecting from a wall
pradakshina path circumambulatory path in a temple
prakara courtyard
prakriti nature, personified as a female
pratoli ornamental gateway
puja the personalised form of worship
purush man; male principle
qawwali one of the nine forms of music in the Hindustani classical system, it was a gift of the Sufi tradition. Qawwals are persons who sing *qawwalis*.
qutb axis; staff
ratha chariot used in religious processions
rekha deul curvilinear towered sanctuary (Orissa)
salabhanjikas tree nymphs
sandhara nali circumambulatory passage around the *garbhagriha*
Sangha the Buddhist community of monks and nuns, founded by the Buddha at Sarnath

Saraswati goddess of learning
shikhara spire
Shiva with Brahma and Vishnu, he is one of the holy Trinity
stupa a dome shaped Buddhist reliquary erected either over sacred relics or to denote a sacred spot or event
surasundaris celestial beauties
Surya the sun god
tala storey
tin tala three-storeyed
tirthankaras preceptors in the Jain religion
torana arched entrance
uttama vimana the pinnacle of the *shikhara* (South India)
uttarapatha northern route
Vamana fifth incarnation of Vishnu as a dwarf
Varaha third incarnation of Vishnu as a boar
vihara Buddhist monastery
Vedas ancient Hindu hymnal books of knowledge
vimana the temple sanctuary as a whole
Vishnu the preserver; one of the Hindu Trinity
zenana ladies' quarters; harem

INDEX

A

B

C

D

QUTB MINAR QU

HUMAYUN'S TOM

AGRA FORT AGRA FO

IAL TAJ MAHAL T

FATEHPUR S

ANCHI SANCHI SANC

KHAJURAHO K

EPHANTA ELEPHA

AJANTA CAVES

ELLORA CAVES

LD GOA OLD GO

PATT

HAMPI HAMPI

RA BRIHADISVAR

KONARAK KON

DARJEELING H